into
the
light

into the light

Edited by Sam Smiles

**An exhibition of French and British painting
from Impressionism to the early 1920s**

Royal Albert Memorial Museum & Art Gallery, Exeter
15 December 2011–11 March 2012

Compton Verney, Warwickshire
31 March–10 June 2012

Sansom &
Company

First published in 2011 by Sansom & Co Ltd.,
81G Pembroke Road, Bristol BS8 3EA

www.sansomandcompany.co.uk
info@sansomandcompany.co.uk

This catalogue has been published to accompany the exhibition
'Into the Light: French and British painting from Impressionism to
the early 1920s' at the Royal Albert Memorial Museum & Art Gallery,
Exeter, 15 December 2011–11 March 2012, and Compton Verney,
Warwickshire, 31 March–10 June 2012

Text © Royal Albert Memorial Museum & Art Gallery, Exeter

ISBN 978-1-906593-77-3

British Library Cataloguing-in-Publication Data:
A catalogue record for this book is available from the British Library

Design and typesetting by E&P Design

Printed by HSW Print Ltd, Tonypandy, Rhondda

Contents

Foreword

It is with great pleasure and a huge sense of achievement that I am writing to introduce *Into the Light*, our inaugural exhibition following the Royal Albert Memorial Museum & Art Gallery's (RAMM) redevelopment.

Closed for four years, we re-open and celebrate the next chapter in RAMM's history with this very special and important temporary exhibition. The City Council is immensely proud of its flagship museum, key to Exeter's role as a regional cultural capital. Councillor colleagues' commitment to the Museum, alongside generous investment from the Heritage Lottery Fund, has made possible this ambitious project to restore, refurbish and extend a remarkable institution.

RAMM has been serving the people of Exeter and beyond for the past 140 years and I would like to congratulate everyone involved – and there are many, who have worked so hard to deliver a project which will ensure that ideas, heritage, identity and creativity continue to be a vibrant part of our shared experience of living, working and enjoying Exeter.

The range and outstanding quality of the paintings that have been brought together to form *Into the Light* is an appropriately splendid way of marking RAMM's re-opening and on behalf of the museum's visitors and of course the City Council, I would like to acknowledge and thank lenders for their generosity in making their work available for this celebratory show: also all of the people who have worked tirelessly behind the scenes to bring this wonderful exhibition to fruition.

Councillor Peter Edwards
Leader of Exeter City Council

Exeter City Council

Preface

Some four years ago a short conversation with Sam Smiles sparked into life an exhibition idea which was conceived as a fitting way to mark the re-opening of the Royal Albert Memorial Museum & Art Gallery (RAMM) after a major development project. From such small beginnings *Into the Light: French and British painting from Impressionism to the early 1920s* has evolved into a major exhibition showing at RAMM, Exeter (15 December 2011 to 11 March 2012) and Compton Verney, Warwickshire (31 March 2012 to 10 June 2012) and this publication.

The initial exhibition idea was a simple one: to bring major Impressionist works to a South West audience. The natural affinity between the South West of England and Brittany provided an obvious starting point to examine Impressionism and its ramifications, but this quickly expanded into a more wide-ranging exploration of the relationship between British and French artists living and working on both sides of the Channel in the late nineteenth and early twentieth century – a subject that has previously received little attention in exhibitions of this kind. The collaboration with Compton Verney has served to bring the topic to an even wider audience.

Over the course of its four years' gestation period, it is Professor Sam Smiles (University of Plymouth) and Penelope Sexton (formerly of RAMM and now of Compton Verney) who have provided the expertise and enthusiasm to turn a good idea into a reality: they both deserve enormous praise for their contributions. At various stages of the project Martin Thomas, Mary Costello and Julien Parsons have all helped to keep things on track; RAMM's exhibition team have delivered the project with their usual skill and dedication amidst all of the competing demands of re-opening a major museum.

Special thanks are due to our funders; our parent body, Exeter City Council and also the Heritage Lottery Fund. Without the support of both this exhibition would not have been possible. Funding from the Association of Art Historians has facilitated some of the research required to put on an exhibition of this magnitude. This is the first time that RAMM has worked with Compton Verney and I hope it will be the start of a fruitful cultural exchange between the South West and the Midlands. This catalogue is testimony to the dedication and professionalism of the team at Sansom & Co; it serves both as a perfect accompaniment to the exhibition and as a stand alone work.

Finally, I should like to extend my sincere thanks to the many institutions and private collectors who have kindly agreed to lending their works of art for the exhibition, and allowing us to include them in this publication.

Camilla Hampshire
Museums Manager
Royal Albert Memorial Museum & Art Gallery

In celebration of RAMM

1868–2011

Into the Light marks the beginning of a new chapter in the story of Exeter's Royal Albert Memorial Museum & Art Gallery, hereafter referred to by its popular and more convenient acronym of RAMM. This exhibition is the first to be seen in the refurbished and extended museum which reopened in 2011 after four years of closure and £24 million of investment. The story of this much-loved institution starts 150 years ago in the wake of a defining moment in Victorian history – the death of Prince Albert in 1861. As Victoria, desperate and racked by grief, withdrew into a period of mourning that lasted until her death 40 years later, her subjects voiced a heart-felt, if not grief-stricken, sympathy for their sovereign's loss. Such a respectful public response was testimony to Albert's achievements, for he was far from a popular figure when he had married the queen two decades earlier: the populace was largely distrustful of a foreigner with a questionable constitutional role, and it took Albert 17 years to earn the title of Prince Consort. The shift in public opinion between 1840 and 1861 owes much to the personal attributes and endeavour of this remarkable man; with no better example of his worth than as the driving force behind the Great Exhibition of 1851. This dizzying display of British colonial might reeled in over six million visitors to Hyde Park and helped define and cement Albert's place in British public life. The death of Albert had another effect, beyond the devastation of the 'Widow of Windsor', and that was to give rise to an array of monuments erected in his honour.

At the time of Albert's demise Exeter's 'great and good' had already been toying with the idea of a museum for several decades. The Devon & Exeter Institution, founded in 1813 and still to be found in Exeter's Cathedral Close, had assembled an eclectic mix of artefacts and specimens gathered by gentlemen, scholars and aesthetes; many of whom had lived or worked abroad and retired to Devon. While the institution's library

flourished, its museum lost impetus. Local naturalists with glass-topped drawers of neatly pinned specimens were eyeing up a new home for their collections. And what to do with Exeter's School of Art which needed new premises? Step forward its president Sir Stafford Northcote. From a well-to-do Devon family, Northcote was Gladstone's private secretary before serving as one of the secretaries for the Great Exhibition; he would go on to have an illustrious parliamentary career as an MP for North Devon, Chancellor of the Exchequer and Foreign Secretary. What better way, Northcote exhorted, for loyal Exeter to commemorate the Consort's life and achievements than founding an institution based on the principles he held so dear – self-improvement and education.

So the Devon & Exeter Albert Memorial was created in 1862. After a campaign had garnered sufficient means through public subscription, an architect was selected, plans drawn up and construction commenced on a new building on land donated to the cause by the local MP. The commissioned architect, John Hayward (1807–91), produced one of the foremost examples of the Gothic Revival style in the South West; its heavy Ruskinian influence leading the architectural historian Dan Cruickshank to liken it to 'an exquisite jewel box... a Venetian casket' sitting in Exeter's Queen Street. The façade of Hayward's museum building remains reassuringly unaltered amidst the modern bustle of shoppers and college students. What goes on behind the façade has changed enormously since it opened in 1868. The library, art school and college that were part of the original nucleus of the Institution matured and flew the nest to form some of the county's most significant cultural and educational assets: Exeter's Central Library, the University of Exeter and the University of Plymouth can all trace elements of their histories back to the Albert Memorial Institution. The museum remained

Reflection and refraction
Anglo-French artistic relations in the nineteenth century

Introduction

The fifty years spanning the 1870s to the 1910s mark a decisive period in the history of European art. Painters found new ways to engage with the contemporary world, both in the subject-matter of their pictures and also, crucially, in the techniques they used. They developed new approaches to the depiction of rural and urban subjects and were concerned to represent contemporary life in its myriad aspects, without idealisation or sentimentality. The pictures they made questioned the conventional understanding of what painting should be: its adherence to traditional themes and its deployment of conventional devices, such as diffuse lighting, subtle half-tones for modelling and a smooth surface finish. Instead, artists began to produce work whose features challenged academic standards, with a more spontaneous response to place and a much more assertive presence of the painted mark. This new orientation included investigations into the representation of light that, ultimately, liberated colour from a merely descriptive function to become instead a means of expression and a key element in pictorial construction. In the history of art these momentous developments are associated primarily with the French art world, especially the transition from Impressionism to Post-Impressionism in the late nineteenth century and the emergence of Fauvism in the early years of the twentieth century. Many artists from abroad took inspiration from this transformation of painting.

The pictures selected for this exhibition exemplify that transition and can be appreciated on that basis alone. But they also prompt further thoughts about the significance of place and about British artists' responses to French painting. With respect to place, the exhibition concentrates exclusively on rural and coastal scenes. At first sight such pictures may seem to depict an alternative to the experience of modern life associated with urban subjects. Indeed the country has often been presented as the antithesis to the city, standing for tradition, conservatism and settled communities rather than the innovation, progressivism and social mobility of the metropolis. Closer examination reveals, however, that the spread of leisure culture and the growth of modern communications in the later nineteenth century blurred such a distinction. The seaside, especially, was in the throes of its transformation from a working environment into a place of recreation for city-dwellers, another site for the expression of bourgeois leisure. In the more remote regions (Cornwall and Brittany, for example), the lives of farming and fishing communities became the object of many painters' fascination, but their work there was made possible by the growth of modern technology, the railway network, and the access it provided.

When considering the British response to French art, how should we position the paintings of these years? In 1922 the influential art critic Frank Rutter looked back over recent developments to declare that 'for the past thirty years our best painters have been following and sometimes – but rarely – developing French traditions...'[1] Rutter's judgement was an orthodox one and for many years this assumption went unchallenged. Recently, however, art historians have investigated the nature of the relationship between British and French art in this period, looking beyond superficial stylistic similarities to examine more deeply the uses to which this new art was put and the contexts in which it was produced and received. This exhibition offers an opportunity to examine work produced on both sides of the English Channel, allowing us to compare the exploration of similar landscapes and to assess the validity of Rutter's opinion. Were British artists merely following in the wake of French

of recent developments in French landscape painting had prioritised certain aesthetic qualities, notably handling and colour, for the art critics writing at the turn of the century. As we shall see, this emphasis helped bring about the reinvention of Constable and Turner as precursors of Impressionism.

Exhibiting French art in England

Artistic traffic flowed from France to England, too.[7] However, awareness of the Impressionists and their successors was very slow to develop in the United Kingdom. This was, in part, because relatively few contemporary works by foreign artists were shown at the Royal Academy and other exhibiting venues in Victorian Britain. As the painter John Lavery recalled, the establishment of the International Society of Painters, Sculptors and Gravers in 1897, with James McNeill Whistler as its first President, helped change the situation:

> Up till our advent there was scarcely a modern foreign picture to be seen on exhibition in England except, perhaps, with dealers. It was considered unpatriotic to include the foreign artists, and we had a hard struggle because few were really interested in Art outside their own country.[8]

The International Society's first exhibition opened in 1898 and included works by Edgar Degas, Édouard Manet, Claude Monet, Jean-Louis Forain, Paul Cézanne, Pierre-Auguste Renoir, Alfred Sisley and Henri de Toulouse-Lautrec, as well as contemporary art from Germany, Italy and the Netherlands. A few Impressionist works were also included in further International Society exhibitions of 1899, 1901 and 1904.

But what of the years prior to 1898; what chance had a young artist or a collector to see contemporary French painting in London? As Lavery notes, French landscape paintings could be seen occasionally at art dealers in London and, less frequently, in public exhibitions. Perhaps because of its affinity with aspects of British landscape painting, the work of some of the Barbizon painters became reasonably familiar to English art-lovers after the 1850s and Jean-François Millet, in particular, was a respected figure. Charles Daubigny, too, had English admirers and visited London in 1866 and 1870–71.[9] The French contribution to the International Exhibition of 1862, held in South Kensington, included paintings by Gustave Courbet, Rosa Bonheur, Jules Breton and other artists with a Realist tendency. Breton's paintings of peasant life remained very popular in England from the 1860s onwards.

It is true, however, that before the International Society was established, there were very few exhibiting venues for contemporary art from abroad. One was the Grosvenor Gallery (1877–90), founded by Sir Coutts Lindsay, which championed progressive art. Famously, the Grosvenor was the occasion for the most notorious contest between tradition and innovation in the British art world, Whistler's libel case against John Ruskin. In 1877 Whistler showed *Nocturne in Black and Gold: The Falling Rocket* (1875; Detroit Institute of Arts) at the Grosvenor. Ruskin objected in violent terms: 'I have seen, and heard, much of Cockney impudence before now; but never expected to hear a coxcomb ask two hundred guineas for flinging a pot of paint in the public's face.' Whistler sued and won his case, but was awarded paltry damages.

Lindsay's taste was wide-ranging. He also supported the rustic naturalist tendency associated with Jules Bastien-Lepage, whose depictions of everyday life in rural northern France were popular in England as they were amongst the British and American art students training in Paris at the Académie Julian in the early 1880s. Bastien-Lepage

JULES DUPRÉ
Crossing the Bridge

1838

Wallace Collection, London

JULES BASTIEN-LEPAGE
Pauvre Fauvette

1881

Art Gallery and Museum Kelvingrove,
Glasgow

visited London on three occasions between
1879 and 1882 and the Grosvenor showed nine
paintings by him (portraits as well as landscapes)
in 1880.[10] This support for contemporary French
art provoked a great deal of critical attention and
it was consolidated by the Grosvenor showing
work by Bastien-Lepage's English followers, Henry
Herbert La Thangue and George Clausen from
1882. The Grosvenor's support for new French
painting was not all-embracing, however. In 1882,
Claude Monet, Camille Pissarro, Eugène Boudin,
Edgar Degas, Pierre-Auguste Renoir, Mary Cassatt,
Berthe Morisot and Alfred Sisley wrote a letter to
Lindsay, requesting the opportunity to mount
a joint exhibition.

> A group of French painters, united by the same
> aesthetic tendencies, struggling for ten years
> against convention and routine to bring back
> art to the scrupulous exact observation of
> nature, applying themselves with passion to
> the rendering of reality of form in movement,
> as well as to the fugitive phenomenon of light,
> cannot forget that it has been preceded in this
> path by a great master of the English school,
> the illustrious Turner.[11]

This application was unsuccessful and when
the Impressionists showed their work in London
the following year it was not at the Grosvenor
but at Dowdeswell's Galleries in New Bond Street,
under the auspices of their dealer Paul Durand-
Ruel. This group show, with the title 'La Société
des Impressionnistes,' was the biggest exhibition
of Impressionism in London before Durand-Ruel's
major presentation of their work in 1905.

The Society of British Artists, established in
1823 but lacklustre through much of the later
nineteenth century, had become a more vital
force after Whistler was elected to it in 1884
and under his Presidency (1886–88) it provided
a further possibility for exhibiting. Monet visited

Whistler in London in 1887 and, at Whistler's invitation, he showed four works at the Society's winter exhibition that year. Another major promoter of contemporary art in London was the New English Art Club, founded in 1886. The membership was drawn up mainly from those young artists who had studied in France and included Philip Wilson Steer, George Clausen and Stanhope Alexander Forbes. In 1888 Degas was one of the exhibitors and the occasional work by some of the Impressionists could be found in NEAC exhibitions over the next decade.

As this review shows, however, in his general characterisation of the late nineteenth-century British art world, Lavery was not mistaken: before the advent of the International Society there was little opportunity for foreign artists to show their work in Britain in public exhibitions and it was indeed the art dealers who provided the British public with much of their exposure to contemporary French painting.[12] The pioneer was Ernest Gambart, who established the French Gallery in Pall Mall in 1854 and in his inaugural exhibition showed work by Barbizon painters and their Romantic predecessors. The French Gallery was not exclusively devoted to overseas artists (many British artists exhibited there, too) but it remained a show-place for European painting into the 1900s.[13] Martin Colnaghi began showing continental pictures in 1881 at the Guardi and Continental Gallery, Haymarket, and established the Marlborough Gallery, Pall Mall, in 1886 for the same purpose. However, neither of these galleries showed Impressionist work. That possibility was afforded primarily by the Parisian dealer Paul Durand-Ruel, the Impressionists' earliest and most committed advocate. In 1870, relocated to London after the outbreak of the Franco-Prussian war, he took out a five-year lease on the German Gallery in New Bond Street and began showing work from what he called the Society of French Artists. His December show in that year included

one work by Monet and two by Pissarro and for the next five years his spring, summer and winter exhibitions usually included one or more paintings by Degas, Manet, Monet, Pissarro, Renoir and Sisley.

Durand-Ruel returned to London in the summer of 1882, showing Degas, Monet, Renoir, Sisley and Cassatt in a gallery in King Street. As already noted, in the following year, he mounted a much more ambitious exhibition at Dowdeswell's Gallery, New Bond Street, with 65 works by Boudin, Cassatt, Degas, Manet, Monet, Pissarro, Renoir and Sisley. In the last decade of the nineteenth century others followed his lead. The Goupil Gallery, in New Bond Street, was the London arm of Goupil & Cie, the most important Parisian art dealers. 20 paintings by Monet were shown at its premises in 1889 and a handful of Impressionist paintings in mixed exhibitions thereafter. Other dealers occasionally showing Impressionist work in the 1890s and 1900s included two establishments in the Bond Street area: the Continental and the Grafton Galleries.[14]

In 1901 Durand-Ruel showed 37 paintings by Monet, Pissarro, Renoir and Sisley at the Hanover Gallery and he mounted another, smaller Impressionist show in London in 1904. His largest London exhibition was at the Grafton Galleries in 1905. It included over 300 works by Boudin, Cézanne, Degas, Manet, Monet, Morisot, Pissarro, Renoir and Sisley. Even at this relatively late date, however, some British reactions were hesitant. In a bid to remind a British readership that advances in art have often been met with puzzlement, Walter Sickert's younger brother, Bernhard, wrote an article in the *Burlington Magazine*, comparing the 'heresies' committed by the Pre-Raphaelite Brotherhood with the Impressionists.[15] *The Times'* reaction was mixed; while granting that the Impressionists' cause was won in Paris and in America, and admitting real excellence in nearly all the exhibitors, the review nevertheless

still found ugliness in Manet, triviality in Degas, and limited range in Monet, despite calling him a genius. Only Renoir and Morisot received unalloyed praise.[16]

French painters and the British scene

Although their work did not find a ready market in the United Kingdom, some of the more significant French painters working in this period visited the country. Monet and Pissarro painted in and around London in 1870 and 1871, Sisley produced a number of Thames landscapes in the summer of 1874, and the following year Morisot painted in the Isle of Wight. Renoir worked in Guernsey in the early autumn of 1883 and Morisot in Jersey in 1886. Sisley visited the Isle of Wight in 1881, although he does not appear to have made any paintings on that occasion; his last British canvases stem from a trip to Penarth and Swansea in 1897. Monet visited London eight times between 1887 and 1904 and produced his atmospheric paintings of the Houses of Parliament, Charing Cross Bridge and Waterloo Bridge from 1899 to 1904. Pissarro returned to England in the summer of 1890, with his son Lucien and the neo-Impressionist Maximilien Luce, painting a variety of London scenes; in 1892 and 1897 he worked in London on two series of paintings at Kew Gardens and Bedford Park, respectively.

The question that arises from the presence of these artists in England is how they reacted to British art and it seems clear that it was the Romantic era, rather than anything later, that attracted the Impressionists. By the 1870s, when Monet and Pissarro made their first visits to London, large numbers of Turner's works, in oils and watercolours, were on public display in the National Gallery and a few of Constable's works were on show there and at South Kensington.[17] Turner was clearly of interest to advanced

French taste. An etching by Félix Bracquemond after Turner's *Rain, Steam and Speed* (1844; National Gallery) was exhibited at the first Impressionist exhibition in Paris in 1874 and, as noted above, Turner's name was invoked in the Impressionists' unsuccessful application to exhibit at the Grosvenor Gallery in 1882. Renoir is reported as saying of the capital's public art collections, '… it was the Turners that first attracted me to London.'[18] Pissarro, likewise, expected his son Lucien to be impressed by the Turner works he saw in London in the mid-1880s.[19] Paul Signac visited London in 1898 to see the Turners and shortly afterwards published *D'Eugène Delacroix au néo-impressionisme* in which Turner is argued to have anticipated not only Impressionism but also the art of Seurat and his followers, such as Signac himself. Pissarro recommended Turner to Henri Matisse who sought out his work on honeymoon in London in 1898. On Matisse's advice, his fellow Fauve André Derain studied Turner when he visited London in 1906.[20]

The origins of Impressionism?

Signac's inclusion of Turner as a precursor of modern painting was not unique. In the years either side of 1900 a number of French but principally British critics began to explore the possibility that British artists might have stimulated advances in French painting.[21] It seemed to be a plausible suggestion, especially as Pissarro's understanding of the importance of English art had recently been relayed in an English journal, *The Artist*: 'It seems to me that we are descended from the English Turner. He was perhaps the first to make his colours shine with natural brilliancy. There is much for us to learn in the English School.'[22] The painter Wynford Dewhurst contacted Pissarro in 1902

ALFRED SISLEY
The Cliff at Penarth, Evening, Low Tide

1897

National Museum of Wales, Cardiff

as he prepared two articles on Impressionism for publication in the art journal *The Studio*. Pissarro provided Dewhurst with reminiscences of his and Monet's reactions to English art in 1870:

> The water-colours and paintings of Turner and Constable, the canvases of Old Crome, have certainly had influence upon us. We admired Gainsborough, Lawrence, Reynolds, &c. but we were struck chiefly by the landscape-painters, who shared more in our aim with regard to 'plein air,' light and fugitive effects.[23]

Dewhurst, however, inferred from Pissarro's testimony not just admiration but instruction as well, suggesting in his articles that Impressionism owed its origins to English painting, notably Constable, the Norwich School, Bonington and Turner. Once the articles were published Pissarro reacted critically and he alerted Dewhurst to his serious reservations:

> I do not think, as you say, that the Impressionists are connected with the English school, for many reasons too long to develop here. It is true that Turner and Constable have been useful to us, as all painters of great talent have; but the base of our art is evidently of French tradition, our masters are Clouet, Nicolas Poussin, Claude Lorrain, the eighteenth century with Chardin, and 1830 with Corot.[24]

Dewhurst was not to be dissuaded, however. Although he included Pissarro's rejoinder in his book *Impressionist Painting: Its Genesis and Development* (1904), he nevertheless declared there: 'Indirectly, Impressionism owes its birth to Constable; and its ultimate glory, the works of Claude Monet, is profoundly inspired by the genius of Turner...it cannot be too clearly understood that the Impressionistic idea is of English birth.'[25] The exhibition of unfinished

paintings, such as *Norham Castle, Sunrise*, at the Tate after 1906 seemed to confim this idea, even though these were works the Impressionists had never seen.[26]

Irrespective of the historical validity of these reconsiderations of Turner, Constable and their contemporaries the fact that such ideas emerged at the turn of the century is indicative of a change in the critical fortunes of Impressionism itself. By the 1880s it was beginning to be acknowledged that in land-scape painting particularly the Impressionist approach had become very influential: 'Impressionism in some form or another is becoming the central idea in a very large proportion of modern picture production. The desire to paint effects rather than subjects is rapidly spreading, and bids fair to grow into the chief motive of our art.'[27] Moreover, from the late 1870s new contributors to art criticism in Britain had begun to talk about colour and form as self-sufficient qualities in painting, irrespective of the ostensible subject-matter of the picture. The so-called 'New Art Criticism' of the 1890s and early 1900s consolidated this approach, emphasising materials and technique when judging works of art.[28] One of these critics was D.S. MacColl who used the opportunity of a major survey of nineteenth-century art in the Glasgow International Exhibition of 1901 to write a book on the course of painting over the last 100 years.[29] In MacColl's view the notable landscape artists on both sides of the Channel, from the Romantic era up to the present, shared a desire to record impressions, always accepting that in France the meaning of Impressionism was more precisely understood than it was in England. MacColl was a critic sensitive to and supportive of modern art in Britain and in France. By reconciling the present with the past he hoped to convince sceptics of the merits of Impressionism.

J.M.W. TURNER
Norham Castle, Sunrise

c.1845

Tate, London

Collecting modern art in Britain

From 1887 to 1905 Impressionist paintings were on show almost every year in at least one exhibition in London, but the prices were comparatively high and very few British collectors bought them.[30] A few works did find buyers, however, and this growth in interest was not restricted to the capital. The pioneer was Captain Henry Hill, a Brighton councillor who bought a Monet and seven works by Degas from the mid-1870s, including Degas' *L'Absinthe* (1875-6; Musée d'Orsay, Paris), at that time known simply as *In a Café*.[31] His collection was auctioned in two sales, in 1889 and 1892, when *L'Absinthe* was acquired by the dealer Alex Reid. Reid had opened the Independent Gallery in Glasgow in 1889, selling work by Degas, Sisley, Monet and others and was influential in the formation of modern collections in Scotland.[32]

By the turn of the century a number of private collectors in Britain had begun to acquire important examples of Impressionist and Post-Impressionist work. Four of these collections, which are all now in public ownership in Ireland and the United Kingdom, demonstrate how what had once been seen as outrageously avant-garde finally became accepted as significant art. The Irishman Hugh Lane entered the firm of Martin Colnaghi in 1893, set up as an art dealer in London in his own right in 1898 and from about 1905 developed a passion for Impressionism. He built up an impressive private collection of modern art which opened to the public in 1908 in temporary premises at Harcourt Street, Dublin. However, controversy over the terms of his will meant that his Impressionist paintings were shown at the Tate Gallery from 1917.[33] William Burrell, a Glasgow shipping magnate, participated in the burgeoning Scottish art market from the 1890s and bought many of his Impressionist works from Alex Reid. He later bequeathed

his collection to Glasgow.[34] Gwendoline and Margaret Davies were Welsh heiresses who began buying works of art in 1908, initially paintings by Turner, Corot and Millet and then by Impressionist and Post-Impressionist artists; by 1924 theirs was the biggest such collection in the country. The Davies bequest is now permanently displayed at the National Museum of Wales, Cardiff.[35] Samuel Courtauld owed his wealth to the textile industry. Having seen the Hugh Lane collection on display at the Tate Gallery, he began collecting in 1922, principally Impressionist and Post-Impressionist works, which he displayed at his London home, 20 Portman Square. He co-founded the Courtauld Institute and made over his collection to it in 1932.[36] In 1923 he set aside £50,000 to buy Impressionist and Post-Impressionist paintings for the national collection.

Yet, in one sense, the accumulation of large collections such as these and the tendency for museums and galleries to show paintings divided up into national schools runs counter to the artistic philosophy of the International Society and, indeed, to the behaviour of artists themselves. In Britain, continental Europe, the United States and Australia variants of Impressionist and Post-Impressionist practice were adopted by numerous artists from the 1880s onwards.[37] The confluence of traditions developed on either side of the English Channel would have been apparent to visitors to the Franco-British exhibition, held in London in 1908. It included works by the French Impressionists and by artists belonging to the New English Art Club, who for over 20 years had sustained a modified Impressionism in England.[38] By placing some of these practices side by side once again, this current exhibition offers the same opportunity to compare and contrast and perhaps to mitigate the over-tidy distinctions of art history.

1 Frank Rutter *Contemporary Artists*, London: Leonard Parsons, 1922, pp. 12–13. Rutter was the art critic for the *Sunday Times*, a supporter of progressive painting and founder of the Allied Artists Association (1908).

2 For British exhibitors in France see Béatrice Crespon 'British Painters in the Paris Salons, 1881–1939: A real presence,' *British Art Journal*, vol. 1, no.2, Spring 2000, pp. 59–61 and Béatrice Crespon-Halotier *Les Peintres Britanniques dans les Salons Parisiens des Origines à 1939*, Dijon: Editions de l'Echelle de Jacob, 2002.

3 See Patrick Noon *Constable to Delacroix: British Art and the French Romantics*, London: Tate Publishing, 2003.

4 For further information on Anglo-French relations in the 1855 Exposition, see Emmanuel Starcky and Laure Chabanne *Napoléon III et la reine Victoria, une visite à l'Exposition universelle de 1855*, Paris: Editions de la Réunion des Musées Nationaux, 2008. See also Stephen Wildman 'Great, Greater? Greatest??: Anglo-French Rivalry at The Great Exhibitions of 1851, 1855 and 1862', *RSA Journal* (Royal Society of Arts), vol. 137, September 1989, pp. 660–64; Marcia Pointon 'Voisins et Alliés: the French and the British at the Exposition Universelle of 1855', *Journal of European Studies*, XI, 1981, pp. 233–61.

5 French criticism was made available to the British reading public in the pages of the *Art Journal*, which published a digest of the reviews of the British exhibits, translated into English. See the *Art Journal*, 1855, pp.229–32, 250–52, 281–83 and 297–300.

6 Armand Dayot *La Peinture Anglaise de ses origins à nos jours*, Paris: L. Laveur, 1908.

7 See Edward Morris *French Art in Nineteenth-Century Britain*, New Haven and London: Yale University Press, 2005.

8 Sir John Lavery *The Life of a Painter*, London: Cassell & Co., 1940, p.111. Lavery was the Society's Vice-President. He had studied in France in the early 1880s, was a follower of Bastien-Lepage, basing his early work on that artist, and, with James Guthrie and others in the so-called Glasgow School, introduced a modified Impressionism to Scotland.

9 In England Barbizon landscapes were collected by James Staats Forbes (Stanhope Forbes' uncle), Alexander Young and Sir John Day. See Sarah Herring 'The National Gallery and the collecting of Barbizon paintings in the early twentieth century', *Journal of the History of Collections*, Volume 13, Issue 1, 2001, pp. 77–89.

10 See Kenneth McConkey 'Rustic Naturalism and the Grosvenor Gallery' in Susan P. Casteras, et al. *The Grosvenor Gallery: A Palace of Art in Victorian England*, New Haven and London: Yale University Press, 1996, pp. 129–45. See also Colleen Denney *At the Temple of Art: the Grosvenor Gallery, 1877-1890*, Cranbury, NJ and London: Associated University Presses, 2000.

11 The letter was also signed by the French battle, animal, and genre painter John Lewis Brown. See Eric Shanes *Impressionist London*, New York: Abbeville Press, 1994, p.173.

12 See Petra ten-Doesschate Chu, 'The Lu(c)re of London: French Artists and Art Dealers in the British Capital, 1859–1914' in *Monet's London: Artists' Reflections on the Thames 1859–1914*, St Petersburg, FL: Museum of Fine Arts, 2005, pp. 39–54.

13 Gambart retired from the French Gallery in 1867 and sold the lease to its manager, Henry Wallis. See Pamela M. Fletcher 'Creating the French Gallery: Ernest Gambart and the Rise of the Commercial Art Gallery in Mid-Victorian London', *Nineteenth-Century Art Worldwide*, vol. 6, no. 1, Spring 2007, ejournal www.nineteenthc-artworldwide.org; also Jeremy Maas, *Gambart: Prince of the Victorian Art World*, London: Barrie and Jenkins, 1975.

14 For a list of these London exhibitions, see Kate Flint (ed.) *Impressionists in England: The Critical Reception*, London: Routledge and Kegan Paul, 1984, pp. 356-75.

15 Bernhard Sickert, 'The Pre-Raphaelite and Impressionist heresies', *Burlington Magazine*, vol. vii, no.26, May 1905, pp. 97–102.

16 'French Art at the Grafton Galleries', *The Times*, 17 January, 1905, p. 6.

17 The Constable collection at South Kensington (now the V&A) was greatly expanded after the bequest of his daughter, Isabel Constable, in 1888.

18 Undated statement quoted in Ambroise Vollard *Auguste Renoir (1841–1919)*, Paris: Paris: G. Crès et Cie 1920, pp. 155–56. It is not known when Renoir visited London, although the early 1880s have been suggested.

19 Letter written 20 February 1883, in John Rewald (ed.) *Camille Pissarro: Letters to his Son Lucien*, London: Kegan Paul, Trench & Trubner, 1943, p. 22.

20 See Rémi Labrusse and Jacqueline Munck 'André Derain in London (1906–07): letters and a sketchbook', *Burlington Magazine*, cxlvi, April 2004 pp 243–60; Rémi Labrusse, Jacqueline Munck et al. *André Derain: The London Paintings*, London: Paul Holberton Publishing, 2006.

21 See Sam Smiles *J.M.W. Turner: the Making of a Modern Artist*, Manchester and New York: Manchester University Press, 2007, chapter 3.

22 *The Artist*, 1 June 1892, vol. 13, p. 190.

23 Letter to Wynford Dewhurst dated 6 November, 1902, published in Wynford Dewhurst 'Impressionist Painting: Second Article', *Studio*, vol. xxix, no. 123, June 1903, p. 94.

24 Letter to Dewhurst, undated, in Wynford Dewhurst *Impressionist Painting: Its Genesis and Development*, London: George Newnes Ltd., 1904, p. 61.

25 Dewhurst *Impressionist Painting*, p. 4.

26 In 1918 Monet talked about Turner: 'at one time I greatly admired Turner; today I care less for him...he didn't shape his colours sufficiently, and he put on too much.' Conversation with Georges Bernheim and René Gimpel dated 28 November, 1918 in René Gimpel (transl. John Rosenberg) *Diary of an Art Dealer*, London: Hodder and Stoughton, 1966, p. 73.

27 *The Artist*, August 1887, vol. vii, p.258.

28 See John Stokes '"It's the Treatment Not the Subject": First principles of the New Art Criticism', in John Stokes *In the Nineties*, Hemel Hempstead: Harvester Wheatsheaf, 1989, pp. 34–52.

29 D.S. MacColl *Nineteenth Century Art*, Glasgow: James Maclehose and Son, 1902.

30 See Flint *Impressionists in England*, p. 8.

31 The painting acquired its modern title when it was exhibited at the Grafton Gallery in 1893. For Hill's collection see Ronald Pickvance 'Henry Hill: An Untypical Victorian Collector', *Apollo* 76, December 1962, pp. 789–91 and Alice Meynell 'Pictures from the Hill Collection,' *Magazine of Art*, 1882, pp. 80–84.

32 Reid had advanced taste and had his portrait painted by

Vincent van Gogh in Paris in 1887. See Ronald Pickvance *A Man of Influence: Alex Reid 1854-1928*, Edinburgh: Scottish Arts Council, 1967. He sold *L'Absinthe* to the director of a Glasgow drapery firm, Arthur Kay. It was exhibited at the Grafton Gallery in London the following year and occasioned a lengthy critical exchange in the press. See Ronald Pickvance 'L'Absinthe in England', *Apollo*, vol. 77, May 1963, pp. 395-98; Kate Flint 'The 'Philistine' and the New Art Critic: J.A. Spender and D.S. MacColl's Debate of 1893', *Victorian Periodicals Review*, vol. 21, no. 1, Spring, 1988, pp. 3–8.

33 Lane was lost at sea when the *Lusitania* was torpedoed in 1915. Years of wrangling followed over whether Dublin or London should have his 39 Impressionist paintings. In 1933, obeying the terms of his bequest, the Dublin Municipal Gallery of Modern Art (now called Dublin City Gallery: The Hugh Lane) opened in Charlemont House, Parnell Square. Since 1993 this gallery now contains most of the disputed paintings. See Barbara Dawson et al. *Hugh Lane: Founder of a Gallery of Modern Art for Ireland*, London: Scala, 2008.

34 The collection was donated to Glasgow in 1944, although it wasn't until 1983 that the collection opened to the public in its current premises. See Frances Fowle et al. *Impressionism and Scotland*, Edinburgh: National Galleries of Scotland, 2008.

35 See Mark Evans 'The Davies sisters of Llandinam and Impressionism for Wales, 1908-1923,' *Journal of the History of Collections*, vol. 16, no. 2, 2004, pp. 219-53.

36 See John House et al. *Impressionism for England: Samuel Courtauld as Patron and Collector*, New Haven and London: Yale University Press, 2004.

37 See Norma Broude (ed.) *World Impressionism: The International Movement 1860-1920*, New York: Harry N. Abrams, Inc., 1990; MaryAnne Stevens and John House (eds) *Post-impressionism: cross-currents in European painting*, London: Royal Academy, 1979.

38 See M.H. Spielmann 'Survey of the Fine Art Section' in Sir Isidore Spielmann *Souvenir of the Fine Art Section: Franco-British Exhibition*, London: British Art Committee, 1908.

The open air
Landscape painting and ruralism in Britain 1880-1914

Between the end of the nineteenth century and the outbreak of the Great War, a vast array of landscape paintings and depictions of rural life were to be observed in commercial and public galleries. The close critical attention paid to these in the review columns of newspapers and periodicals, and the parallel growth in the circulation of photographic images of rural scenery, as well as prints and illustrated rural guide-books, all bore witness to what was in effect an expanding and evolving culture of ruralism within British society.

The roots of this particular culture lie in the period of the 1880s, where this exhibition begins. Paintings by George Clausen and Henry Herbert La Thangue from the start of that decade under-line contemporary fascination not just with the landscape, but with the lives and customs of the rural worker. This was a period when the effects of agricultural depression brought about through a combination of bad weather, poor harvests and the influx of cheap American grain imports accounted for a continuous process of rural depopulation. At the same time, the develop-ment of new forms of mechanised production meant that traditional rural customs were fast disappearing from the countryside. In such a context any reminders of time-honoured, harsh but noble forms of existence and of honest toil in the fields were to be widely savoured. Clausen's paintings of sturdy field-workers therefore take their place alongside nostalgic accounts of country life by poets and writers of the period like, for example, Richard Jefferies, whose 1885 natural history book *The Open Air* upheld the redemptive powers of nature.[1] Countless critics, notably the turn of the century liberal politician C.F.G. Masterman, produced lengthy discourses on the incessant growth of the city and the harmful effects of city life upon the moral and physical character of urban workers.[2] Against this background, rather idealised images of their rural counterparts

provided some reassurance that the racial stock and the backbone of the national culture was not, or need not be, inevitably in decline. Underlying the period was the deep conviction about the purity and superiority of rural life over that of the city which fuelled the Arts and Crafts, Back to the Land and Simple Life movements as well as preservation societies like the National Trust, founded in 1895, and periodicals such as *Country Life*, launched in 1897.

A fascination with authentic, unsophisticated modes of life far from overly-cultivated urban centres was not of course exclusive to Britain in the latter part of the nineteenth century. There are parallels to be observed in many European and North American contexts. In this respect the decision of so many younger British painters to complete their art training not in the Royal Academy schools, which were increasingly regarded as stiflingly conservative in their practices and their curriculum, but in the more informal private ateliers of France and Belgium, is especially significant.

Following brief stints at the Government Art School or the Royal Academy, George Clausen, Henry Herbert La Thangue and Alexander Stanhope Forbes all completed their training in Paris in the early 1880s. Of particular concern for these painters, as for numerous ex-patriot students in Paris at this time, were what appeared to be the startlingly realist plein-air studies of the lives of the peasantry in northern France produced by the artist Jules Bastien-Lepage, who died in 1884. The impact of Bastien-Lepage drew many of these younger artists in their vacations to coastal locations like Cancale, Concarneau and Quimperlé in Brittany, there to pursue the French painter's direct method of working out of doors; his subjects placed before him in conditions of steady grey light. For Clausen, La Thangue and Forbes, this appeared to be a revolutionary method resulting in an honest and detached

JEAN-FRANÇOIS MILLET
Summer, the Gleaners

1853

British Museum

document of everyday customs in remote coastal communities.[3] The results they perceived as a complete contrast to the slick and formulaic forms of painting – mythological nudes, or 'fancy-dress' re-creations of scenes from ancient Greece or Rome – which were still a staple ingredient at Royal Academy summer exhibitions and still regarded as a measure of aspiration in the tuition of younger artists.

On their return from France, Clausen, La Thangue and Philip Wilson Steer were all founder members of the New English Art Club in 1886 (initially to be titled the 'Anglo-French exhibiting society') and a characteristic style of highly detailed sombre tonal realism dominated the Club's output in its first two years. Public taste responded well to these exhibitions, although some of Clausen's harsher representations of female field workers were considered unacceptable by a public disturbed by their overt evidence of the de-feminising effects of a life of toil in the open fields; as seen to some degree in his *Winter's Work*, 1883–84. Along with other British artists such as the Sussex painter, Edward Stott, Clausen's development from the later 1880s and 90s was to be towards the more poetic, elegiac quality associated with the French painter Jean-François Millet who was widely appreciated amongst British audiences and critics of the period. Millet's works became especially popular following Julia Cartwright's 1896 biography which further underscored a nostalgic, at times melancholic hankering after a disappearing rural idyll.[4] Millet's effect on Clausen resulted in less detailed observations of a particular individual in a specific social context and in more monumental compositions in which the rural worker becomes more readily a timeless and heroic figure of popular memory.

In pursuit of the type of subjects and a similar quality of light he had observed in northern France, Stanhope Forbes was an early member of what became known as the Newlyn School, an artists' colony established in the Cornish fishing village from the mid-1880s. For Forbes, Newlyn was 'an English Concarneau'. While both James McNeill Whistler and Walter Sickert had produced atmospheric, impressionist seascapes in St Ives in 1883–34, it was the working lives of the fishing community that preoccupied the Newlyn painters, exemplified by Forbes' most ambitious and influential work *A Fish Sale on a Cornish Beach*, popularly received by audiences at the Royal Academy in 1885 who appreciated its painstaking detail and skilled observation. Thus began the growing appeal of Cornwall as a painting destination; an exotic and remote location far from the metropolitan centre, but also more accessible through the developing rail networks which drew not just painters, but increasingly tourists too. At the very moment, then, when Cornwall was being opened up to mass tourism at the end of the nineteenth century, its image was becoming ubiquitous at Royal Academy exhibitions. Cornwall in fact emerged as an ideal site upon which to reflect modern, urban anxieties about moral and physical decline. Within this context a distinctive identity for the county was constructed, asserting its separateness from the vulgar materialism of the metropolis, emphasising its position at the nation's edge and its pre-industrial past; a site both of curious folklore and ancient customs. Alongside other painters like Frank Bramley and Thomas Cooper Gotch, Forbes' paintings of old Newlyn, the harbour and surrounding scenery 'framed' Cornwall for tourists in the 1890s; the composition of his paintings essentially reappeared in countless postcards, popular prints and illustrations – all of which depict a pre-modern location unaffected by change and progress.

By 1908 however, the date of Laura Knight's painting *The Beach*, the emphasis of the 1880s and 90s on enduring hardship and relentless toil had clearly shifted to reflect a county now increasingly associated with a sun-filled atmosphere of recreation, with picturesque rituals like Forbes' own *Gala Day* (Hartlepool Museum) of 1907, or with simple holiday pleasures and signs of the beneficial effects of sunlight and fresh air – a constant feature in Edwardian discourse on health and fitness.

A shift in representations from the countryside as site of labour to one of pleasure and leisure had already registered in the work of Steer. Only briefly attracted in the early 1880s to the square brush technique of Bastien-Lepage, Steer's represent-ations of another artists' colony, Walberswick on the East Anglian coast, were strikingly advanced in British art for their day, mingling the fluidity of handling of Whistler with the more intense colour of Claude Monet and at times the neo-Impressionist technique of Georges Seurat and Camille Pissarro. Steer's seemingly spontaneous depictions of carefree young girls cavorting on the beach offended many of the more conservative critics of the later 1880s as overtly crude and un-naturalistic, but in a manner typical of this artist, sensuous pleasure in a sun-filled seaside location was here expressed by the most appropriate technique. Within a very few years and after a striking change in his style and technique, Steer would be regarded as the rightful descendent of J.M.W. Turner and John Constable, both of whom were perceived by the early 1900s – with distinctly nationalist overtones – as the 'true' progenitors of Impressionism.[5] Framed at that time within imperialist discourse, Steer's rolling panoramic vistas of the Wye and Severn Valley and of North Yorkshire were widely perceived by many at the turn of the century as icons of Englishness and frequently found a place in overseas collections.

If claiming British antecedents for the basis of the Impressionist technique preoccupied some writers, for many painters the immediate

focus was upon French Impressionism itself. A lightening of the palette and a concern with more transitory atmospheric effects and seasonal conditions was clearly evident in Clausen's *A Frosty March Morning*, of 1904. By this point and after the growing representation of the artists in London galleries, the influence of Monet and Pissarro was no longer quite the worrying sign of overt radicalism in contemporary British art, something that is reflected perhaps in Clausen's appointment as Professor of Painting at the Royal Academy that same year.

A typically Impressionist subject, the observation of seasonal effects, concerns two paintings in the present exhibition of apple trees in blossom in the French countryside. The first of 1893 by the Australian Charles Conder, a friend of William Rothenstein from the Académie Julian, reveals the artist's admiration for Monet's lightened palette. In the second painting however, produced in the same year, Armand Guillaumin's more intense colour, sinuous, rhythmic line and decorative effect points instead to the influence of his friend Vincent van Gogh. The paintings we now associate with Post-Impressionism marked something of a reaction against Impressionism, increasingly regarded in this period as excessively objective and naturalistic. While Post-Impressionism was to have little impact on paintings of the British rural scene in the 1890s, the Irish artist Roderic O'Conor was an exception. An early admirer of both van Gogh and Paul Gauguin, he spent time at Pont-Aven in Gauguin's circle in 1892. O'Conor's *Yellow Landscape*, a result of that particular visit, witnesses the artist's more subjective and intuitive response to the landscape, conveyed through ribboned, expressive brushwork. The artists' colony at Pont-Aven, like that at Newlyn, was also predicated on an ideal of a group of artists intermingling with an authentic rural community, one whose daily lives provided a constant store of subjects to be represented in varying degrees of naturalism or increasingly with imaginative interpretation. The relations between the artists' practice and wider forms of cultural tourism have been widely discussed.[6]

The Celtic Renaissance of the 1890s and a wave of contemporary studies of and popular fascination with myth and folklore were also to underpin interest in coastal communities: in Cornwall, in Brittany, and also in the 'artists' town' of Kirkcudbright on the west coast of lowland Scotland, where legend and local archaeology fuelled visitors' interests in what they perceived as the poetic atmosphere and mystery of the region.[7] The Scots artist Samuel Peploe was to paint regularly at Kirkcudbright and further north in the Western isles in the period following the First World War. But far less detained by Celtic culture and poetic symbolism, he and his friend J.D. Fergusson worked in 1910 at Royan, further down the Atlantic coast from Pont-Aven and near to Bordeaux. Royan was already a fashionable tourist resort at this point and it was the modernity and hedonistic pleasures of the scenery, of day and night, that both artists observed, resulting in their transition from at first a Whistlerian handling of paint towards the brighter colour and simplified forms of Henri Matisse and André Derain, whose works Fergusson had seen while he was exhibiting at the Salon d'Automne in Paris in October 1907.

That 1907 Salon d'Automne also contained Paul Cézanne's memorial exhibition and from this date and especially through Roger Fry's two major exhibitions at the Grafton Galleries in London in 1910 and 1911–12, younger British artists were increasingly exposed and receptive to the works of Cézanne, Matisse, Gauguin and van Gogh, despite persistent hostility from many. For these younger artists the bright colouring, rhythmic handling and vitality of the artists Fry termed Post-Impressionists provided a welcome contrast

PHILIP WILSON STEER
Richmond Castle

1903

Tate Britain

to what the critic Laurence Binyon described as the 'picnic landscapes' perpetually on display at Academy exhibitions.[8] These landscapes, once, and still for many, regarded as soothing consolation, were for others now excessively nostalgic and mawkishly sentimental evocations of the English countryside. They were exemplified by the formulaic output of such artists as Benjamin Williams Leader and John Arnesby Brown and to some extent too in the modified Impressionist handling and by now familiar subjects of Clausen and La Thangue. A critical shift occurs in the writings of Binyon and Fry by 1910 in which the word 'atmosphere' is replaced by 'rhythm' as the approved quality of a work of art, to be achieved by removing unnecessary and distracting detail and paring a composition down to its essential characteristics.[9] These processes, typical of early modernism, were accompanied by a corresponding shift in the artists' choice of location.

The growing importance of Matisse and Derain would encourage what amounted to a revision of aesthetic geographies after 1910, and corresponded to that developing taste for more sensuous and pleasurable landscapes. The Welsh artist Augustus John also represents something of this new tendency in his desire for elemental, remote and 'southern' or Mediterranean land-scapes and particular physical types. The result was a series of depictions of his partner Dorelia and their extended family decoratively grouped on the shores of the Étang de Berre near Martigues in Provence. Shown in the Chelsea Chenil Gallery in 1910, at the same time as Fry's first Post-Impressionist exhibition, John's works represent a very obvious shift in terms of formal technique from those of Clausen, and yet there are nevertheless fundamental similarities in their representation of healthy, vigorous types to be found in locations far from the physically and morally weakening conditions of urban and suburban life.

With its extreme simplicity indebted to Matisse, Vanessa Bell's 1912 painting *Studland Beach* advanced the development towards abstraction in early twentieth-century British art through a radical rejection of detail. The work's severe flattening of form and colour and total elimination of atmosphere appears to conform to the criteria of 'significant form' as espoused by her husband, and Roger Fry's ally, the critic Clive Bell. In this the artist is encouraged not to imitate, but to find an 'equivalent for life', and to seek above all to arouse a disinterested aesthetic emotion in the viewer.[10] Irrelevant factual detail and atmospheric effect would inevitably detract from this emotion. Such a reductive aesthetic was especially well-attuned to the austere simplicity of line and flat expanse of colour of this section of Studland Bay in Dorset. Studland had been the site of Bell family holidays and had occasioned a series of paintings by the artist from 1909. Lisa Tickner's study of Bell's painting points to the open sweep of the beach as signifying both a masculine Romantic, sublime and sensory space for con-templation of the self, and a feminine, domestic space associated with mothers and young children.[11] The work carries a specific auto-biographical significance for Bell, as well as wider social and cultural meanings associated with the Edwardian era. To this end, Tickner argues, it can be seen as a 'distillation', rather than a rejection of the everyday and a close correlation can be observed between the characteristic formal qualities of early modernism and the experience of modernity. Similar correlations can be seen in the paintings of landscapes and rural scenes by artists most usually associated with the Camden Town Group, with the painter Spencer Gore in particular.

Between 1900 and 1914 the population of London had continued to swell and the suburbs to expand, to the disdain of many. H.G. Wells' 1909 novel *Tono-Bungay*, for example, presented

a typical account of suburbia as: 'Endless streets of undistinguished houses, undistinguished industries, shabby families, second-rate shops, inexplicable people who in a once fashionable phrase do not "exist"'.[12] Wells' comment betrays a snobbish distaste for what many perceived to be the tawdry vulgarity of suburban life. Beyond that particular impulse, overcrowding, unsanitary housing conditions and a potentially worrying degree of worker unrest had for some time pre-occupied social reformists, most famously Charles Booth who published *Life and Labour of the People in London*, 17 volumes of which had appeared between 1889–1903.

One potential solution to these urban problems was the development of the Garden City Movement. Led by Ebenezer Howard, author of the influential 1902 study, *Garden Cities of Tomorrow*, the principles of the movement were the creation of new towns on the model of traditional village communities, with houses designed according to Arts and Crafts principles.[13] With proper amenities, but set within easy access to fields and woodland, garden cities such as Letchworth in Hertfordshire, originally to be named 'Ruralsville', were fundamentally utopian solutions intended to unite the best of city and country life.

Such a utopian ideal informs Spencer Gore's painting *The Cinder Path* of 1912. Along with Walter Sickert, Gore had been a member of the Camden Town Group since it formed the previous year, 1911, and a resident of that same north London suburb where he painted interior subjects of his wife and domestic servants and views down over quiet parks and back gardens from first and second floor windows. From August to November 1912 his fellow Camden Town painter Harold Gilman rented his Letchworth house to Gore and his young family. By this point Gore had moved on from the early influence of his Slade tutor Philip Wilson Steer's landscape style and also from the Impressionist handling of his close

friend and associate Lucien Pissarro. Following his exposure to Derain, Cézanne, and the two Fauve painters, Auguste Herbin and Othon Friesz, whose works also appeared in copies of *Rhythm* magazine, Gore's painting style began to change. His Letchworth paintings remain generally faithful to the scene, but as one of his most advanced works, *The Beanfield*, demonstrates, they underline formal, structural relationships and deploy vibrant non-naturalistic colour – most notably here in the zigzag geometric patterns at the bottom edge of the canvas – all for the purpose of expressing what he himself termed 'the emotional significance which lies in things'.[14]

The Cinder Path, a view of the edge of the town where the Garden City merges harmoniously into the countryside, represents a rather different ruralism to that associated with Clausen, Forbes and La Thangue in the 1880s. Gore's Letchworth paintings, like the landscapes here of his Camden Town associates – Robert Bevan's *Devonshire Valley, no. 1* and Charles Ginner's *Clayhidon, 1913*[15] – do not focus our attention on the condition of the rural worker or fisherman, rather they produce a modern, pleasurable vision of ancient and once wild but now cultivated landscapes – secured within a rhythmic pattern of fields and hedgerows.

In the years immediately before 1914 the countryside becomes ever more accessible to the city-dweller, primarily through an increased availability of transport. From the development of suburban train lines, better connections to national networks and, after 1911, the rapid increase in motor car sales, the rise in tourism of all kinds corresponds to the growth of leisure and social aspiration. At the same time the countryside was ever more visible in the city, not simply in the constant presence and popularity of landscape exhibitions, but through the wider circulation of different forms of visual imagery. Crucial in this respect was the proliferation of travel posters displayed at railway and under-

VINCENT VAN GOGH
A Wheatfield, with Cypresses

1889

National Gallery, London

ground tube stations after 1908. This period sees the rise of the poster artist, with the importance of the profession frequently celebrated in art magazines like *The Studio,* itself a powerful proponent of shifting forms of ruralism since its beginnings in 1893. Poster designers like Walter Spradbery and Fred Taylor, who both featured in its pages, were employed by travel companies to entice customers to rural locations or seaside resorts and, benefiting from advances in colour lithography, they adopted vibrant and decorative Post-Impressionist forms in order to convey the pleasurable benefits of healthy countryside and fresh air.[16] There was no place within this visual imagery for melancholic lament or retrospective regret about vanishing ways of life; instead the rhythmic designs and flat colours of Matisse and the Fauves are combined to present a modern ideal of the countryside, the experience of which was now easily available through modern forms of transport and communication.

It would be wrong, however, to conclude that these new aesthetic responses to the landscape displaced the approaches typical of the art produced at the turn of the century. The New English Art Club and Royal Academy exhibitions continued throughout the interwar years to display works by George Clausen, who maintained the luminous palette of Monet and the subjects and formal compositions typical of Millet in poetic evocations of English rural life and labour of the kind he had realised by 1900. Others, like Wynford Dewhurst in his 1919 *Summer Mist, Valley of La Creuse* combined the example of Monet with Turner in the production of idyllic atmospheric views, here of the French countryside. All of which points to the continued co-existence of diverse forms of landscape painting throughout this entire period and denies any straightforward sense of art historical progression. That plethora of styles suited to a variety of tastes also reflects the specialism and differentiation common within modern consumer markets. It also clearly underlines the extent to which varied responses to the countryside in late-nineteenth and early twentieth-century Britain were continually mediated through artistic reactions to early, primarily French modernism.

1 Richard Jefferies, *The Open Air*, London: Chatto and Windus, 1885.
2 For example, *The Heart of the Empire, Discussions of Modern City Life in England*, London: Fisher Unwin, 1902.
3 For discussion of the importance of Bastien-Lepage for this particular generation of artists, see 'Figures and Fields' in Kenneth McConkey, *British Impressionism*, Oxford: Phaidon, 1989.
4 Julia Cartwright, *Jean François Millet: his life and letters*, London: S. Sonnenschein; New York: Macmillan, 1896.
5 Wynford Dewhurst's *Impressionist Painting: its Genesis and Development* of 1904 was one of those studies to cite Turner's influence on the Impressionists in particular.
6 See for example Griselda Pollock and Fred Orton, 'Les Données Bretonnantes: La Prairie de Représentation' in F Frascina and C Harrison *Modern Art and Modernism: A Critical Anthology* London: Harper Row and the Open University, 1983, and Nina Lübbren, *Rural Artists' Colonies in Europe, 1870-1910*, Manchester: Manchester University Press, 2001.
7 On Celticism and artists in Kirkcudbright see Ysanne Holt, '"The Veriest Poem of Art in Nature": E.A. Hornel's Japanese Garden in the Scottish Borders', *Tate Papers*, Autumn, 2004.
8 Laurence Binyon, *The Saturday Review*, 31 December 1910, p.840.
9 *Rhythm* was also the title of the magazine founded by John Middleton Murry and Michael Sadleir in 1911 and J.D. Fergusson was its art editor.
10 Bell espoused these views most famously in his book *Art* of 1914.
11 See 'Vanessa Bell: *Studland Beach*, Domesticity and "Significant Form"' in Lisa Tickner, *Modern Life and Modern Subjects: British Art in the Early 20th Century*, New Haven & London: Yale University Press, 2000. Part of the discussion here draws on Alain Corbin's *The Lure of the Sea: The Discovery of the Seaside in the Western World, 1750–1840*, Berkeley and Los Angeles: University of California Press, 1994.
12 H.G. Wells, *Tono-Bungay*, London: Macmillan, 1909.
13 Ebenezer Howard's ideals developed in part from his reading of the 1888 utopian novel by American writer, Edward Bellamy, *Looking Backward* and were first aired in 1898 in *Tomorrow: A Peaceful Path to Real Reform*, reissued as *Garden Cities of Tomorrow* in 1902. For more discussion of Gore's paintings of Letchworth see Ysanne Holt, 'An Ideal Modernity: Spencer Gore at Letchworth', in *British Artists and the Modernist Landscape*, Aldershot: Ashgate, 2003.
14 Spencer Gore, 'Cezanne, Gauguin, Van Gogh &c., at the Grafton Galleries', *Art News*, 15 Dec 1910, pp.19–20.
15 For more on the paintings Bevan and Ginner produced around ex-Slade student Harold Harrison's farm Applehayes in Devon, see Rosalind Billingham, *Artists at Applehayes: Camden Town Painters at a West Country Farm, 1909-24*, Herbert Art Gallery and Museum, Coventry, 1986, see also Sam Smiles, (ed.) *Going Modern and Being British, Architecture and Design in Devon*, Exeter: Intellect Books, 1998.
16 On the rise of the poster artist see Catherine Flood, 'Pictorial Posters in Britain at the Turn of the Twentieth Century', in David Bownes and Oliver Green, (eds), *London Transport Posters: A Century of Art and Design*, London: Lund Humphries, 2008.

For more discussion of this shift in ruralism and the effects of greater visibility of and access to the countryside in the years just prior to 1914 see my essay 'The Camden Town Group goes to the Country' in *Tate Research: The Camden Town Group*, Tate on-line research project, 2011.

Vanessa Bell
1879–1961

Studland Beach

c.1912
oil on canvas
76.2 x 101.6 cm

Tate, London

In 1901 Bell was accepted as a student at the Royal Academy Schools and adopted a competent naturalist style in her early work, showing her admiration for Whistler and John Singer Sargent. In 1910, however, she was profoundly affected by the paintings she saw at the exhibition organised by Roger Fry at the Grafton Galleries, *Manet and the Post-Impressionists*: 'Here was a sudden pointing to a possible path, a sudden liberation and encouragement to feel for oneself which was absolutely overwhelming.'[1]

With her husband, Clive Bell, the art critic, she had holidayed at Studland Beach in Dorset in 1909 and returned there in 1910 and 1911. In 1909 she had painted the beach under Whistler's influence, but her paintings of the 1910s are strikingly different. With their simplified forms and bold use of colour, they have an obvious affinity to Post-Impressionist and Fauvist developments.

Modern critics have observed that Bell may have been responding to three bathing scenes exhibited by Fry in 1910, especially Maurice Denis' *Grandes Baigneuses*. However, as with Steer (*The Beach at Walberswick*) and Laura Knight (*The Beach*) before her, Bell eschews the potential of the beach to stage an idealised presentation of the naked figure and concentrates instead on the everyday and self-contained world of women, children and modern leisure.[2]

1 Vanessa Bell 'Memoir' VI' (unpublished MS), quoted in Frances Spalding *Vanessa Bell*, London: Weidenfeld and Nicolson, 1983, p.92.
2 It has also been suggested that the figures around the bathing tent in the background evoke Piero della Francesca's *Madonna della Misericordia* (1460–62; Pinacoteca Comunale, Sansepolcro). See Spalding, *Vanessa Bell*, pp.100–113; Lisa Tickner 'Vanessa Bell: Studland Beach, Domesticity, and "Significant Form"', *Representations*, no. 65, Special Issue: *New Perspectives in British Studies*, winter, 1999, pp. 63–92.

Robert Polhill Bevan

1865–1925

Devonshire Valley, no. 1

c.1913
oil on canvas
51.2 x 61.2 cm

Royal Albert Memorial Museum & Art Gallery, Exeter

Bevan had studied in London in 1888 and then at the Académie Julian in Paris. He visited Brittany in the early 1890s, where he was part of Gauguin's circle. The lithographs he made there may have been influenced by his friend Roderic O'Conor, whose work at that time used strong linear patterning. On return to England Bevan spent three years on Exmoor making prints of hunting scenes. His first one-man show in 1905, at the Baillie Gallery in Bayswater, was too advanced for English taste and for the next few years he modified his style. The establishment of the Allied Artists' Association in 1908 offered him the chance to show his work without compromise. Bevan also joined the Fitzroy Street Group of artists, presided over by Walter Sickert. Here he associated with Sickert, Spencer Gore, Charles Ginner, Lucien Pissarro, Harold Gilman and others who established the Camden Town Group (1911–12) and its successor the London Group (founded in 1913) as rival exhibiting societies to the Royal Academy and the waning New English Art Club.

With Gore and Ginner, Bevan spent time painting landscapes in the West Country, at Applehayes Farm, near Clayhidon on the Devon and Somerset border.[1] Its owner Harold Bertram Harrison had studied at the Slade School of Fine Art as a mature student in the 1890s. He bought the farm in 1909 and equipped it with studios, inviting Slade students to Devon between 1909 and 1916. Bevan stayed there in 1912, 1913 and 1915, rented lodgings nearby for the next four summers and again in 1922 and bought his own property in the area in 1923.

Bevan's work in the 1910s is marked by the influence of Post-Impressionist painting, which he had not only experienced in Brittany but also in exhibitions in London, especially *Manet and the Post-Impressionists* (Grafton Galleries, 1910) and *Cézanne and Gauguin* (Stafford Gallery, 1911). Between 1912 and 1914 he was also influenced by the French Cubist painter André Lhote and derived from him the idea of composing with complex patterns of interlocking planes.[2]

1 See Rosalind Billingham, *Artists at Applehayes: Camden Town Painters at a West Country Farm 1909–1924*, Coventry: Herbert Art Gallery, 1986.
2 Lhote's work was included in Roger Fry's second Post-Impressionist exhibition in 1912, but it may have been first introduced to Bevan by Frank Rutter, who also exhibited one of Lhote's paintings in the *Post-Impressionist and Futurist Exhibition* (Doré Galleries, 1915). See John Yeates 'Robert Bevan and the Cumberland Market Group' in Tim Craven *A Countryman in Town: Robert Bevan and the Cumberland Market Group*, Southampton: Southampton City Art Gallery, 2008, p.43.

A Breton valley

c.1894
lithograph

British Museum

The Chestnut Tree

c.1916–19
oil on canvas
50 x 60 cm

Ashmolean Museum, Oxford

Green Devon

1919
oil on canvas
44.5 x 54.8 cm

Plymouth City Museum
and Art Gallery

Eugène Louis Boudin

1824–1898

A Beach near Trouville

1895
oil on canvas
54.3 x 81.2 cm

The Barber Institute of Fine Arts,
University of Birmingham

Deauville and Trouville are situated a few miles west of Le Havre either side of the estuary of the river Touques. Trouville's development as a resort started in the 1830s, when the English fashion of sea bathing was imported to Normandy. A railway station at Trouville opened in 1863, bringing the coast within easy reach of Parisians. The Duc de Morny, Napoléon III's half-brother, developed Deauville in the 1860s. Fashionable amenities included a grand hotel, luxury villas, a hippodrome and a centre for hydrotherapy and other cures.

Boudin is customarily seen as an important precursor for Impressionism because of his commitment to painting *en plein air*. He be-friended Monet in the late 1850s and joined the Impressionists in their first exhibition in 1874. He first painted at Trouville in 1861 and over the next 35 years made over 300 paintings showing holiday-makers on the beaches of the two resorts. In 1884 he built a house at Deauville which became his principal residence.

Boudin had married a Breton girl, Marie-Anne Guédès in 1863. His grief at her death in 1889 caused him to reconsider his painting, finding solace in nature, rather than the crowds of holidaymakers that had typified his art hitherto.[1] He painted large canvasses, almost empty of figures, where the sky and the play of light over the seashore constitute the subject. Perhaps it was these naturalistic concerns that caused him to pay special attention to an exhibition of English paintings in Paris in 1894, at the Galerie Sedelmeyer, which he described as '...an extremely interesting exhibition of the English school. Turner, Constable, and others. I derived much benefit from this exhibition... there is a serious lesson for us.'[2]

1 Letters to his Le Havre friend Ferdinand Martin, dated 24 and 28 March 1889, quoted in G. Jean-Aubry, *Eugène Boudin*, Neuchatel: Éditions Ides et Calendes, [1968], 1977, p. 110.
2 See letter to Louis Braquaval, dated June 1894, quoted in Laurent Manoeuvre, 'Eugène Boudin, entre tradition et modernité' in *Eugène Boudin en Normandie*, Honfleur: Musée Eugène Boudin, 1998, p. 13.

Deauville

1893
oil on canvas
50.8 x 74.2 cm

The Courtauld Gallery, London
(on display at RAMM only)

George Clausen
1852–1944

A Frosty March Morning

1904
oil on canvas
63.5 x 76.2 cm

Tate, London

Clausen trained in London and then briefly in Paris at the Académie Julian (1882). He was a founder member of the New English Art Club (1886), whose members were the most responsive to developments in French painting. Like many young English artists, Clausen admired Jules Bastien-Lepage and met him when he was in London in the early 1880s. Bastien-Lepage was noted for his tenacity in painting the rural community of Damvillers, a place he knew intimately, rather than generalising about rural life.[1] Clausen, likewise, made a close association with the landscapes near his home, showing a similar commitment to particular localities, their inhabitants and life on the land.

Winter Work (overleaf) was painted at Childwick Green, Hertfordshire, where Clausen lived from 1881 to 1884 and it demonstrates his wish to leave the studio behind to paint directly from nature and, most importantly, to document the activities of a gang of field labourers by eschewing professional models and painting the actual members of this rural community. The work in question is the preparation of beets for sheep fodder.

A Frosty March Morning was painted at Widdington, Essex, Clausen's home from 1891 to 1905.[2] The works he painted there show a greater interest in atmosphere and effects of light, as Clausen incorporated some of the advances made by the Impressionists. In 1904 he became Professor of Painting at the Royal Academy, a post he held for two years. Speaking to the students about painting in the open air he declared that a landscape 'should not be so much an inventory as a transcript or translation of a mood of nature.'[3]

1 See Kenneth McConkey, *Sir George Clausen RA, 1852–1944*, Bradford and Tyne and Wear Museums, 1980,
2 The picture has sometimes been known as *The Allotment Garden, Winter.*
3 'Landscape and Open-Air Painting' in George Clausen *Six Lectures on Painting*, London: Elliot Stock, 1904, p. 95.

An artist painting out of doors

1882
oil on panel
21 x 12.1 cm

Bristol's Museums, Galleries and Archives

Winter Work

1883–34
oil on canvas
77.5 x 92.1 cm

Tate, London

INTO THE LIGHT **49**

Charles Conder

1868–1909

**Apple Blossom
at Dennemont**

1893
oil on canvas
73 x 60 cm

Ashmolean Museum, Oxford

Conder's youthful work in and around Melbourne in the late 1880s was engaged with contemporary interests, especially the rendering of sunlight and the depiction of modern life, and showed a sophisticated awareness of the work of Whistler, Japanese art and other current tendencies. He arrived in Paris in 1890. Initially he considered the Impressionists to be too radical and was more impressed with the work of Bastien-Lepage. By 1891, however, he was responding to Puvis de Chavannes and especially to Whistler and Monet. He met Henri de Toulouse-Lautrec and Louis Anquetin and with Anquetin sketched in Normandy that spring. Anquetin was turning away from his experimental work of the 1880s, when he had used flat areas of colour surrounded by thick, black outlines, and was now urging a return to more traditional craft skills. He was very influential on Conder, who began to adopt a more luxurious use of colour and a looser handling than he had in Australia.

Conder returned to Normandy in 1892, staying some six months first at Dennemont, near Mantes, then in the hamlet of Chantemesle on the Seine upstream of Vétheuil, and finally in Vétheuil itself with Anquetin. Monet had painted in this area in the 1870s and early 1880s and Conder, like many British and American art students, was deliberately retracing the older man's footsteps.

The artist and critic D.S. MacColl was in Paris to review the annual Salon for the *Spectator* – he compared Conder to Corot and befriended him. Through MacColl Conder was introduced to the civil servant James Granville Legge who bought this picture.[1]

1 See Ann Galbally *Charles Conder – the last bohemian*, Carlton South, Victoria: Melbourne University Press, 2002.

Wynford Dewhurst

1864–1941

Summer Mist, Valley of La Creuse

c.1919
oil on canvas
65.2 x 81.1 cm

National Museum of Wales, Cardiff

Dewhurst was born in Manchester and after abandoning his intended career as a lawyer trained at the École des Beaux-Arts, in Paris. The first Impressionist work he may have seen was a painting by the Belgian artist Émile Claus in the Maddocks Collection in Bradford, but his travels in France exposed him to many more. He was in contact with Claus and with Maxime Maufra, another Impressionist follower, and also corresponded with Pissarro in 1902 but it was Monet above all who inspired his art. In 1904 Dewhurst published a book dedicated to Monet: *Impressionist Painting: Its Genesis and Development.* It was one of the first major studies of the movement in English and a pioneering venture in many respects. However, it has become notorious for his insistence, which was shared by many of his contemporaries, that the English landscape tradition, especially the work of Constable and Turner, was at the root of modern French painting.

This picture demonstrates very clearly the hold Monet had on Dewhurst's approach to landscape. Monet had painted fourteen canvases in this area in the winter and early spring of 1888–89 and Dewhurst's painting may be regarded as something of a tribute to his example. In the 1900s Dewhurst's handling and heightened colour became quite noticeable features of his work, as here, but they lacked the aesthetic coherence that underpinned the advances Monet and others had made.

John Duncan Fergusson

1874–1961

Twilight, Royan

1910
oil on board
27 x 34.9 cm

Scottish National Gallery
of Modern Art, Edinburgh

In the mid-1890s Fergusson was accepted by the Trustees' Academy, Edinburgh, but abandoned formal training after a few months and was effectively self-taught. Initially he painted after Whistler, but regular trips to Paris from 1897 exposed him to the work of the French Impressionists. Around 1900 he met S.J. Peploe and with him took regular summer tours to the fashionable resorts of Brittany and Normandy, painting *en plein air* to capture light effects. In 1907 Fergusson moved to France and stayed there until the outbreak of the Great War in 1914. He developed a great admiration for Matisse, exhibited regularly with the Salon d'Automne, established in 1903 for showing progressive art, and associated with André Dunoyer de Segonzac and Fauvists such as Othon Friesz and André Derain.

In 1909 and 1910 Fergusson spent the summers with Peploe at Royan, a very fashionable resort on the Gironde estuary, north of Bordeaux. A number of his pictures were painted at twilight when the overall tonality of the scene is relatively subdued, emphasising the residual colour. The strong outlines of the boats and sails provide a rhythm to the surface organisation of the picture, in tune with Fergusson's and others' contemporary interest in this quality in painting.[1]

1 Fergusson was the Art Editor for the periodical *Rhythm* established by John Middleton Murry and Michael Sadler in London in 1913.

Stanhope Alexander Forbes

1857–1947

A Fish Sale on a Cornish Beach

1885
oil on canvas
123.5 x 155.6 cm

Plymouth City Museum
and Art Gallery

Forbes was born in Dublin. He studied art at the Lambeth School of Art and the Royal Academy, then in Paris under Léon Bonnat. He responded enthusiastically to French instruction, commenting that he got twice as much work done in Paris and that 'very few of us in England work hard enough or stick long enough at the training.'[1]

In 1881 Forbes went to Brittany with his fellow artist Henry La Thangue, both of them now committed to working *en plein air*, following the example of Jules Bastien-Lepage. Forbes found himself struggling with the problems of recording scrupulously the scene in front of him:

> There is always some difficulty cropping up. Either the model doesn't turn up or the day changes from cloudy effects to bright sunlight or vice versa and we find ourselves camped out on a spot ready to begin to paint when suddenly the whole scene changes...life goes on from day to day with occasional varieties of trouble in the form of wind which blows your canvass down every instant or covers you with dust, nuisances in the form of dirty children and worse which I need not describe...[2]

Forbes' major painting from that trip was *A Street in Brittany*, exhibited at the Royal Academy and bought by the Walker Art Gallery, Liverpool the following year. This early success convinced Forbes to pursue outdoor painting rather than portraiture as his specialism. He returned to Brittany with La Thangue in 1882, working at Quimperlé where he painted *The Convent* (p.59). His uncle, James Staats Forbes, who was an important collector of naturalist pictures, had an option on the picture but Forbes convinced him to allow the Bradford collector John Maddocks to purchase it instead, where it joined La Thangue's *Boat Building Yard*, painted the previous year.

Forbes arrived in Newlyn in January 1884 and joined the artists' colony established there by

Walter Langley and others two years previously.[3] His *Study of a Fisherwoman* (p.58) was one of the first paintings he completed as he applied the lessons he had learned in Brittany to this 'English Concarneau'. This sketch was part of his preparations for the very ambitious *Fish Sale on a Cornish Beach* which he would exhibit at the Royal Academy in 1885 with great success. He described his progress on the picture to his mother in July 1884:

> I am painting a very large picture again this year, quite different to anything I have ever done and with hardly one touch of blue in it and it is giving me a woeful lot of trouble. There will be lots of girls in it, fish fags we call them here, fish boats, sea, sky etc.[4]

The artists of the Newlyn School are associated above all with their representation of a close-knit working community, living a simple and traditional life at the extreme edge of England. But, as with Gauguin's interpretation of Brittany in the same period, this was a partial truth. By the 1880s the railway system had improved access from Cornwall to the rest of England, supporting the farming, clay and mineral industries as well as making it easy for artists to send their pictures to London. The network also encouraged tourism and some of the more picturesque villages were developing as resorts. Forbes' small sketch, *Beach Scene – St Ives* (p.58), shows something of the relaxed life of the holidaymakers there, in stark contrast to the world of work depicted in the *Fish Sale* from a year earlier.

1 Letter to his mother, dated 17 May [1880]. Tate Gallery Archive TGA 9015.2.1.67.
2 Letter to his mother, dated 31 July [1881], Cancale. Tate Gallery Archive TGA 9015.2.1103.
3 Alice Meynell, 'Newlyn', *Art Journal* April 1889, pp. 97–102. In this important article Meynell identified the group as making a distinctive contribution to the contemporary art world.
4 Letter dated 6 July [1884], c/o Mrs Henry Maddern, Bellevue, Newlyn, Penzance, Cornwall. Private collection.

Beach Scene – St Ives

1886
oil on canvas
19 x 29 cm

Bristol's Museums,
Galleries and Archives

Study of a Fisherwoman

1884
oil on canvas
15 x 20 cm

Penlee House Museum
& Gallery

The Convent

1882
oil on canvas
86.5 x 76 cm

private collection

Paul Gauguin

1848–1903

Landscape at Pont-Aven

1888
oil on canvas
66.1 x 100 cm

The Barber Institute of Fine Arts,
University of Birmingham

This picture, ascribed to Paul Gauguin, shows Lollichon Field and Pont-Aven church, in southern Brittany, a familiar sight for Gauguin as it was close by the Pension Gloanec, where he lodged on his visits to Pont-Aven in 1886 and 1888.

The composition can be compared to a painting by Gauguin, signed and dated 1886, which shows a very similar view but from a marginally closer viewpoint.[1] Compared with the 1886 picture, this version has a 'transitional' appearance from Gauguin's work in the middle 1880s, when his art was still heavily indebted to his mentor Camille Pissarro, towards a more adventurous style, with emphatic brushwork and a more forceful use of colour both visible. Nevertheless, the picture provokes a number of questions. Although some pictures of 1888 show that Gauguin had not dispensed entirely with Impressionism, most of his paintings of that year are more evidently concerned with a simplification of nature.[2] It is also unclear why he would wish to produce what is essentially a slightly modified copy of the 1886 picture.

1 *Lollichon Field and the Church of Pont-Aven*, sold Christie's 4 February 2002. Private collection. A related view is *The Field of Derout-Lollichon* (1886; Los Angeles County Museum of Art).
2 Compare Gauguin's treatment of this field and farmhouse in *Breton Girls Dancing, Pont Aven* (1888; National Gallery of Art, Washington).

Charles Ginner

1878–1952

Clayhidon

1913
oil on canvas
38.4 x 63.9 cm

Royal Albert Memorial Museum
& Art Gallery, Exeter

Ginner was born in Cannes, to British parents. He trained in France and did not settle in England until 1909. Like his colleagues Robert Bevan and Spencer Gore, he became a member of the Camden Town and London groups in the 1910s. He worked at Clayhidon in Devon in 1912, 1913 and 1914.[1] Like Bevan he did not work *en plein air* but made sketches and studies which he worked up into finished pictures, a practice intensified after 1911 when Sickert showed him how to work from squared drawings.[2]

Ginner's paintings are clearly indebted to Post-Impressionist examples, sometimes borrowing from van Gogh, at other times, as here, taking inspiration from the followers of Gauguin, using emphatic bounding contours to separate forms and to exaggerate surface pattern. The small fields of the Devon countryside, with their characteristic hedgerows, lent themselves very well to this interest in pattern-making, and the viewpoint Ginner has adopted, omitting the sky, reinforces this effect. As the foreground and middle-ground of this painting demonstrate, one of Ginner's techniques was the regular application of thick paint, a process which tends to concentrate the spectator's attention on the surface but which can also give his pictures a rather laboured appearance.

This painting was first exhibited in the 1913 exhibition at Brighton City Art Gallery, *English Post-Impressionists, Cubists and Others*, which included the work of many Camden Town artists.

1 For Clayhidon see under Robert Bevan.
2 John Rothenstein *Modern English Painters*, vol. 1, London: Macdonald [third edition], 1984, p. 201.

Spencer Frederick Gore

1878–1914

The Beanfield, Letchworth

1912
oil on canvas
30.5 x 40.6 cm

Tate, London

Gore trained at the Slade School of Fine Art, 1896–99. In 1904 and 1905 he painted in northern France, where he met Sickert and absorbed the influence of French painting. With Sickert, Lucien Pissarro, Robert Bevan, Charles Ginner, Harold Gilman and others he established the Fitzroy Street Group in 1907 and the Camden Town Group in 1911. Roger Fry's first Post-Impressionist exhibition (1910) and the Stafford Gallery's 'Cézanne and Gauguin' exhibition (1911) caused him to reconsider his allegiance to Impressionism and to adopt a technique that used areas of unmodulated colour constructively.

The Gore family spent August to November 1912 in Harold Gilman's house at Letchworth, Hertfordshire, the garden city north of London developed from 1903. The paintings Gore produced there were some of his most progressive. By comparison with its preparatory drawing (British Museum) *The Cinder Path* (p.66–7) uses colour more deliberately to flatten perspective.[1] *The Beanfield* is even more obviously composed in terms of non-naturalistic coloured areas, highlighted by the zig-zag pattern in the foreground representing bean plants.

Gore's work at Letchworth demonstrates the extent to which British art had been transformed over the past 30 years. By coincidence, George Clausen had painted *Winter Work* at Childwick Green, some 20 miles south of Letchworth. If Clausen's naturalism represents the earlier British response to cross-Channel influences and Gore's Post-Impressionism the later, we can also consider the two worlds they depict: traditional agricultural husbandry in a quiet hamlet, painted in the 1880s, and the outskirts of a planned new town, painted in the 1910s.

1 *The Cinder Path* exists in three versions. This painting was formerly owned by Gore's colleague, Robert Bevan; the Tate's larger version was shown in Roger Fry's second Post-Impressionist exhibition in 1912.

***Study for
The Cinder Path***

1912
coloured chalks and
graphite on paper,
squared for transfer
23.5 x 33.2 cm

British Museum

facing page

The Cinder Path

1912
oil on canvas
35 x 40 cm

The Ashmolean Museum,
Oxford

Armand Guillaumin

1841–1927

Les Pommiers à Damiette

1893
oil on canvas
100 x 116.5 cm

Aberdeen Art Gallery & Museums

Guillaumin worked as a railway official before studying at the Académie Suisse in 1861. There, he met Paul Cézanne and Camille Pissarro in 1864, with whom he maintained lifelong friendships. He exhibited at the Salon des Refusés in 1863 and at six of the eight Impressionist exhibitions.

It is reported that Guillaumin always painted landscapes *en plein air* and did not retouch his canvases in the studio. His exuberant colour and strong sense of design mark him out as a distinctive artistic personality. As a result, some have called him a precursor of Fauvism.[1] His distinctive use of colour is accounted for by his artistic friendships of the 1880s which included van Gogh, Seurat and Signac. Reviewing the 1881 Impressionist exhibition J-K Huysmans said of him:

> M. Guillaumin is also a colourist, and what is more, a ferocious colourist. At first his canvases seem to be a dog's dinner (margouillis) of competing tones and of crude contours, a cluster of zebra stripes in vermillion and Prussian blue. But blink your eyes and everything falls into place, the drawing firms up, the screaming tones subside, the hostile colours are reconciled and we are amazed by the unanticipated delicacy exhibited in parts of his paintings.[2]

Damiette is a village in the Yvette valley near the town of Orsay, south west of Paris. Guillaumin first worked there in 1883–84. However, the apple trees in the foreground, referred to in the title, also appear in works bearing the names of other nearby locations, Saint-Chéron and Miregaudon.[3]

1 *Armand Guillaumin (1841–1927): l'impressioniste fauve*, Chatou: Musée Fournaise, 2003.
2 J-K Huysmans 'L'exposition des indépendants' in *L'Art Moderne*, Paris: G. Charpentier, 1883, p.261.
3 See Georges Serret and Dominique Fabiani, *Armand Guillaumin, 1841–1927, Catalogue raisonné de l'oeuvre peint*, Paris: Editions Mayer, 1971.

Laura Knight

1877–1970

The Beach

c.1908
oil on canvas
127.5 x 153 cm

Laing Art Gallery, Newcastle upon Tyne
(on display at RAMM only)

Laura Knight lost her father when she was six and was brought up by her mother in difficult financial circumstances. She trained at the Nottingham School of Art from the age of 13. At the turn of the century she moved to Staithes, near Whitby, whose community of artists can be compared with those at Newlyn, St Ives and Walberswick in this period. With her artist husband Harold she moved to Cornwall in 1907, the couple basing themselves in the neighbourhood of Newlyn and joining the artists' colony there. Responding to the distinctive light of the region, and working *en plein air*, Laura Knight began to paint in a style that leaned towards Impressionism, combining bright colour with more vigorous brushwork.

The Beach is often regarded as inaugurating Knight's work in Cornwall, with many subsequent paintings similarly devoted to the subject of women and children's leisure activities in bright sunlight. This tendency reflects the fact that Cornwall was by now a popular holiday destination as much as it was a working community. The beach in Stanhope Forbes' *Fish Sale* (1885), painted just over twenty years earlier and on a similarly grand scale, makes a sober contrast to the world of gaiety and pleasure evoked by Knight. In Forbes' painting the shore is a stage on which is played out an aspect of adult working life; in Knight's picture the beach has become effectively a domestic space, thronged with children at play.

Henry Herbert La Thangue

1859–1929

The Boat Builder's Yard, Cancale, Brittany

1881
oil on canvas
76.1 x 82.2 cm

National Maritime Museum, London

La Thangue was born in London and studied painting at Lambeth School of Art and then the Royal Academy (1874–79). He won a three-year scholarship to Paris, studying at the Ecole des Beaux-Arts, where he came under the influence of Bastien-Lepage and other adherents of rustic naturalism. He spent the summer of 1881 at Cancale in Brittany with his fellow student Stanhope Forbes, painting *en plein air* and utilising the square-brush technique associated with Bastien-Lepage.

Forbes' correspondence with his mother in 1881 indicates that there was 'a want of sympathy' between the two artists, which made them colleagues rather than friends. Nevertheless, he valued La Thangue's professionalism highly:

> In the working way he is invaluable from every point of view. I share his ideas and admire his work just sufficiently not to fall into imitation. I emulate his industry which is his strongest point.[1]

The Boat Builder's Yard was the major painting resulting from this campaign of work. It shows the benefit of working *en plein air*, capturing the fall of bright sunlight, although the young woman wearing Breton dress and clogs is somewhat awkwardly introduced, posing as opposed to engaging in any meaningful activity.

The picture was exhibited at the Grosvenor Gallery in 1882 and helped establish La Thangue's reputation. It was bought by the Bradford industrialist John Maddocks who also purchased Forbes' *The Convent*, as well as works by Clausen and by French artists associated with rustic naturalism.[2]

1 Letter dated 31 July, Cancale. Tate Gallery Archive TGA 9015.2.1.103.
2 See Butler Wood, 'The Maddocks Collection at Bradford', *The Magazine of Art*, 1891, pp.304–6. In 1881 Maddocks offered to buy all La Thangue's pictures for two years in return for a fixed income but was declined. See Caroline Fox and Francis Greenacre, *Painting in Newlyn 1880–1930*, London: Barbican Art Gallery, 1985, p.102 note 18.

Claude Monet

1840–1926

**The Museum
at Le Havre**

1873
oil on canvas
75 x 100 cm

The National Gallery, London

Monet was living at Argenteuil for most of the 1870s but he also paid visits to his home town Le Havre and painted views of the harbour in 1872, 1873 and 1877. The picture that gave the Impressionists their name, *Impression Sunrise* (1872; Musée Marmottan), was one of them. It was shown at the first Impressionist exhibition, rousing the critic Louis Leroy to title his review in *Le Charivari* (25 April 1874), 'The Exhibition of the Impressionists'.

The Museum at Le Havre shows the inner harbour looking across to the Musée des Beaux-Arts, built in 1845, at a time when the town was developing its capacity as a trans-Atlantic port. The museum's neo-classical facade was designed to impress, but in Monet's treatment the jumble of masts and spars imposes a workaday rhythm on to this emblem of civic pride. The handling is very varied, with broken brushstroke in the rippling water of the foreground set against larger areas of relatively solid colour in the hulls and sails at the quayside. The muted tonal scheme is true to overcast northern light and its greys and dull ochres momentarily dominate the touches of green, orange, vermilion and blue with which Monet has animated the surface.

Between 1878 and 1881 Monet lived in Vétheuil on the Seine. He was in serious financial difficulty and could no longer afford to live in Argenteuil. His troubles were tragically compounded by the death of his wife, Camille Doncieux in September 1879. He painted over a hundred canvases of the town and the river. The church features in many of them and its appearance in all seasons and at different times of day brings to mind the Rouen Cathedral series of the 1890s.

The Church at Vétheuil may have been painted in midstream, either from the small island there or from the floating studio Monet had brought with him from Argenteuil. It was probably painted *en plein air* in a single sitting and shows how effectively Monet's technique had matured to capture the full intensity of sunlight. He has taken some care to model the church, such that its mixture of Romanesque and Renaissance architectural elements are clearly discernible. The sky, in contrast, is rendered with a thin layer of blue applied unevenly, allowing the ground layer to show through. The separation of the individual touches of pigment in the water allows Monet to represent mobile, shimmering reflections with brilliant success.

The Church at Vétheuil

1880
oil on canvas
79.2 x 68.5 cm

Southampton City Art Gallery

Claude Monet

Roderic O'Conor
1860–1940

Yellow Landscape

1892
oil on canvas
67.6 x 91.8 cm

Tate, London

O'Conor was born in County Roscommon. He studied in Dublin before attending the Académie Royale des Beaux-Arts in Antwerp (1883–4). He returned to Ireland briefly, but moved to Paris in 1886 to study there and resided in France for the rest of his life. In the early years of the twentieth century he was a familiar figure in Parisian circles, a friend of the critic Clive Bell and of Somerset Maugham, who based on him the artist Clutton in *Of Human Bondage* (1915). A private income freed O'Conor from the obligation to sell his paintings which meant that few of them were in circulation and his achievement was obscured until 1956, when the sale of his widow's estate brought his work back to critical attention.

His early paintings show the influence of Sisley and Monet, but in 1890 he adopted a Divisionist style. He probably visited Brittany for the first time in 1887 and returned there from autumn 1891 to March 1893. Gauguin was in Tahiti at the time (O'Conor's friendship with him developed either in Paris in late 1893 or in Brittany the following year) but O'Conor became friendly with his followers, especially Armand Séguin and the Scot Eric Forbes-Robertson, who was a friend of Robert Bevan. O'Conor met Emile Bernard for the first time in 1892. Bernard had just organised a van Gogh exhibition in Paris and seems to have brought some of these pictures to Pont-Aven.[1] O'Conor was deeply affected by van Gogh and his work of 1892 reflects that influence strongly, especially a series of paintings of cornfields.

Yellow Landscape is very thickly painted throughout, using non-naturalistic colour (pink and green in the sky, red and blue in the shadows) and rhythmic mark-making to respond to the landscape expressively. The alternating stripes of vivid colour produce the sensation of summer's heat and glaring light.

[1] Jonathan Benington, *Roderic O'Conor. A biography with a catalogue of his work*, Dublin: Irish Academic Press, 1992, pp.49–52.

Samuel John Peploe
1871–1935

Boats at Royan

1910
oil on board
27 x 34.9 cm

Scottish National Gallery
of Modern Art, Edinburgh

In the 1890s Peploe studied painting in Edinburgh and then in Paris, where he was influenced by the paintings of Emile Bernard and Maurice Denis. As well as still-lifes, interiors and figure studies, he also painted landscapes *en plein air* in Scotland, which owe a considerable debt to Pissarro and Sisley in their handling of paint. From 1904 he worked alongside J.D. Fergusson on painting holidays in Islay, Brittany and Normandy. He moved to Paris in 1910, returning to Edinburgh in 1912. In Paris he exhibited at the Salon d'Automne and mixed with progressive artists, including Othon Friesz and Jules Pascin.

Peploe spent the summers of 1910 and 1911 at Royan, working with Fergusson. The town had a reputation as one of the most elegant seaside resorts in France and was popular with wealthy holiday-makers. In this picture Peploe shows the extent to which his earlier Impressionist-derived style has been modified by his experience of more recent painting. While his use of colour and perspective are both still essentially naturalistic, the handling of the paint is more expressive and gestural. As with all his mature work, Peploe's interest in drawing underpins the composition, using naturally occurring linear features to outline and reserve areas of colour.

Like Fergusson, Peploe was associated with the Rhythm group and exhibited with them in 1912 at the Stafford Gallery in London. Because of their interest in colour and expressive, almost Fauvist approach to painting, both painters, together with their contemporaries Francis Cadell and Leslie Hunter, have subsequently been referred to as the Scottish Colourists.

Louveciennes

1870
oil on canvas
45.8 x 55.7 cm

Southampton City Art Gallery

Lucien Pissarro

1863–1944

**Apple Blossom,
Riversbridge Farm,
Blackpool**

1921
oil on canvas
53.3 x 64.8 cm

Royal Albert Memorial Museum
& Art Gallery, Exeter

Lucien Pissarro was Camille Pissarro's eldest son.
He was born in France and studied with his father.
In the mid-1880s, with Camille, he responded to
the work of the neo-Impressionists Seurat and
Signac, as seen in their contributions to the eighth
Impressionist exhibition of 1886. He settled in
London in 1890, becoming a British citizen in 1916.

Because of his intimate knowledge of the
Impressionist movement, Lucien Pissarro was an
important link between the French and British
art worlds and was able to speak with authority
about the tenets of the new painting. He divided
tones by applying pigment in touches of separate
colour and his palette, with its absence of black,
was an example to his English colleagues. He was
associated with the Fitzroy Street Group around
Walter Sickert and was one of the founders of the
Camden Town Group of artists. In 1919, with the
painter and Tate Gallery curator James Bolivar
Manson, he formed the short-lived Monarro
Group, whose title was derived from the names
of Claude Monet and Camille Pissarro.

Blackpool is a small village in South Devon.
Pissarro had painted in nearby Dartmouth in
March 1913, returned to the area in 1921 and
would do so again in 1922. In letters to his wife
written in April 1921 he complained that he had
yet to find any blossom to paint, but by June
the apple trees had bloomed and he made this
picture to record the scene.

Pierre-Auguste Renoir

1841–1919

Moulin Huet Bay, Guernsey

c.1883
oil on canvas
29.2 x 54 cm

The National Gallery, London

Renoir travelled frequently in the early 1880s, including Normandy, the Mediterranean, Italy and Algeria. In 1883 he stayed one month in Guernsey, from early September to 9 October. From his lodgings in St Peter Port he made regular excursions to Moulin Huet bay, about three miles away in the south-east of the island, and painted 15 canvases of this subject.[1]

Two of his letters from Guernsey survive. One, dated 27 September, is to Durand-Ruel and provides valuable information about his activities there.[2] Two significant points emerge from this letter. First, Renoir distinguishes between the two types of pictures that he has produced on the island: 'paintings' and 'documents' from which paintings can be made on his return to Paris. This picture was probably painted entirely on site, however: a 'painting' rather than a 'document'. Its handling is very energetic, painted wet in wet, with highly varied brushstrokes throughout, orientated to the major contours of the natural features.

Second, in choosing to paint the beach and its bathers Renoir was engaging with a contemporary scene, but he was clearly also thinking of a very wide frame of cultural reference. Thus, he tells Durand-Ruel about the lack of bathing cabins and the need to change among the rocks, both men and women mixed. The result, he claims, is more like being in a picture by Watteau than in reality. As in Athens, he notes, women don't worry about men being nearby and even young English girls aren't shy when disturbed as they get ready to bathe. These remarks were no doubt intended, in part, as jocular observations but the references to Watteau and Athens also reflect the impact of Renoir's trip to Italy in 1881 and his growing sympathy for artistic tradition and the classical understanding of the human body in nature.

In the late 1880s Renoir developed rheumatoid arthritis and from the mid-1890s spent increasing amounts of time at Cagnes-sur-mer, on the Mediterranean coast, buying a house there in 1907. St Tropez is some 60 miles further west. The Neo-Impressionist painter Henri-Edmond Cross had moved to nearby Cabasson in 1891 and a year later, on his recommendation, Paul Signac settled in St Tropez. Signac described the coast in similar terms to the romanticised image of Brittany that had been in circulation a decade earlier: distant and culturally distinctive from Paris and peopled by a simple folk whose way of life repudiated the over-sophisticated lifestyle of the metropolis. Following Seurat's untimely death in 1892 Signac emerged as the leader of the Neo-Impressionist movement and numerous artists visited St Tropez and painted there, although its isolation made it difficult to reach except by boat. Renoir's painting does not betray any influence of Neo-Impressionism, however. This sketch is painted in long, fluid brushstrokes, with no evidence of pointillist dots or colour division.

1 Two of these canvases were shown in Durand-Ruel's 1905 London exhibition of Impressionist paintings.
2 The other, dated 5 September, mentions Robinson Crusoe and the writer Victor Hugo, who stayed in Guernsey from 1855–70 in self-imposed exile from the regime of Louis Napoleon. For an excellent analysis of Renoir's work on Guernsey see John House, *Renoir à Guernesey*, States of Guernsey: Guernsey Museum & Art Gallery, 1988.

St Tropez

c.1898–1900
oil on canvas
54.5 x 65.4 cm

Birmingham City Art Gallery

Walter Sickert

1860–1942

Rushford Mill, Chagford

1916
oil on canvas
63.8 x 76.5 cm

The Fitzwilliam Museum, Cambridge

Sickert was born in Munich, to German and English parents, who settled in England shortly afterwards. His father was a graphic artist and encouraged his son's artistic bent, but Sickert's first career was as an actor touring provincial theatres. He had met Whistler by at least 1879 and became his assistant in 1882, after leaving the Slade School of Fine Art where he had studied for a few months in 1881–82. With Mortimer Menpes, he accompanied Whistler to St Ives in the winter of 1883–84. Menpes records Sickert making several oil sketches a day but only a few have been identified.[1] Clodgy Point is the headland beyond the promontory depicted in Whistler's *Cliffs and Breakers* and Sickert's sketch is very obviously indebted to Whistler's example. He exhibited the painting at the Society of British Artists exhibition in 1885.

Earlier in 1883 Sickert had met Degas for the first time, the artist who would replace Whistler as his most important inspiration and who became his lifelong friend. From 1898 to 1905 he lived in France, exhibiting his work there. On his return to London Sickert shared his knowledge of recent French painting with younger artists, such as Robert Bevan, Spencer Gore, Charles Ginner and Lucien Pissarro who came to his studio for discussion and exhibited together as the Fitzroy Street Group, later known as the Camden Town Group (1911–12).

Like Degas, Sickert is primarily known for his urban scenes and social observation but he did not neglect landscape painting. He visited Chagford, in Devon, on at least two occasions in the 1910s and produced numerous studies and paintings of the town and its environs. *Rushford Mill*, was not painted *en plein air* but worked up in the studio from small oil sketches and detailed drawings.[2]

1 *On the Sands, St Ives*; *Beach Scene, Cornwall*; and *Beach Scene*. Ref. Wendy Baron, *Sickert: Paintings and Drawings*, London: Phaidon, 2006, cat.15, and nos. 1 and 2 under cat. 16, p.152.
2 An oil study (15 x 24 cm) for the stepping stones in this picture was sold at Sotheby's 23 November 2006; lot 63. Ref. Wendy Baron, *Sickert*, p.445, listed under cat.479.

Clodgy Point, Cornwall

1883–84
oil on panel
12.3 x 21.5 cm

Hunterian Museum & Art Gallery, University of Glasgow

Alfred Sisley

1839–1899

**La Petite Place –
La Rue du Village**

1874
oil on canvas
42.5 x 55.2 cm

Aberdeen Art Gallery
& Museums

Sisley was born in Paris to English parents, but made his career in France. Of all the Impressionists he was the one who concentrated most exclusively on landscape. In 1874, the year this canvas was painted, he participated in the first Impressionist exhibition and then made a four-month trip to England, painting scenes on the Thames. He returned to France in October. With its depiction of autumnal foliage, this painting was presumably painted soon after he arrived back in Louveciennes, his residence at the time.

Sisley's understanding of seasonal change is notable here, showing how the pallid light of an overcast day in autumn produces soft shadows and a limited overall tonal range. In its very modesty, the picture exemplifies one of the most distinctive features of Impressionism, the avoidance of a sentimental approach to the rural world and in its place a disciplined examination of the actual appearance of places.

Philip Wilson Steer

1860–1942

Although artists did not usually stay all year round at Walberswick, the Suffolk fishing village had developed a reputation as a good sketching ground in the mid-1880s. Many of its summer visitors, like Steer, were Paris-trained and committed to painting *en plein air*.

Steer studied at the Gloucester School of Art and then at the South Kensington Drawing Schools (1880–81). Rejected by the Royal Academy, he enrolled at the Académie Julian, and then in the École des Beaux Arts between 1882 and 1884.[1] It is unclear how much progressive art he saw in France, although large exhibitions devoted to Monet in 1883 and Manet in 1884 were available to him; he would also have been able to see Impressionist works at dealers in London. He was one of the founder members of the New English Art Club in 1886, whose original title was The Society of Anglo-French Painters; with Sickert he organised the breakaway group, The London Impressionists, whose single show took place in December 1889.

By at least 1888 Steer was the leading interpreter of French Impressionism in England. His Impressionism, however, was idiosyncratic. He used bright, unmixed colours to produce flickering light effects but he tied his technique to observable facts. Thus, the pebbly beach,

ripples and reflections at Walberswick lent themselves to a variegated response, with a multitude of touches of colour. Close inspection of *The Beach at Walberswick* (overleaf), for example, reveals touches of blue, red and yellow in the sea and sand but these accents are not organised systematically in a pointillist manner.[2]

Steer's work in these years stands out as a radical intervention in English art. His paintings did not sell, however, and by the late 1890s he had realigned his practice with the tradition of landscape that went back to Turner and Constable.

1 He left because he didn't pass the compulsory French examination.
2 Steer's sketchbook in the Victoria and Albert Museum (E275-1943; titled 'mostly Walberwswick') has a preparatory drawing for this on pp. 30–31 including brief colour notes. A second sketchbook (E297-1943; titled 'Walberswick', p. 20) has a preliminary design for *Walberswick, Children Paddling*.

Two girls on Walberswick Beach, Suffolk

c.1888–89
oil on panel
25.1 x 35.2 cm

Plymouth City Museum
and Art Gallery

**The Beach at
Walberswick**

c.1889
oil on wood
60.3 x 76.1 cm

Tate, London

facing page

**Walberswick,
Children Paddling**

1891
oil on canvas
64.3 x 92.6 cm

The Fitzwilliam Museum,
Cambridge

Henry Scott Tuke
1858–1929

July Sun

1913
oil on canvas,
53.4 x 43.5 cm

Royal Academy of Arts

Tuke's family moved to Falmouth shortly after he was born. He was encouraged to draw and paint from his youth and in 1875 he enrolled in the Slade School of Fine Art in London. He then spent two years in Paris (1881–83) where he met Jules Bastien-Lepage who encouraged painting *en plein air*. He worked in Newlyn from 1883 to 1885 before returning to Falmouth where he spent the rest of his life.

Although he also painted a range of portraits, genre scenes and marines, Tuke is best known for his portraits of naked young men, bathing or sun-bathing. Some paintings were completed in his studio but he preferred to work in the open air, asserting that 'the truth and beauty of flesh in sunlight by the sea' couldn't be captured indoors. For models he used neighbours, family friends and members of the local community. Tuke's work was well received at the Royal Academy and he was elected to full membership in 1914.

Tuke recorded that he had painted *July Sun* 'practically in one sitting'[1] and, although it was a study, he felt it was complete enough to exhibit at the Royal Academy summer exhibition in 1914. The model was Nicola Lucciani. Unlike Tuke's normal sitters he was a professional model and it is possible that Tuke had met him in London when teaching at the Royal Academy Schools in January 1913. Lucciani died on active service in 1916 and Tuke donated the picture to the Royal Academy the following year.[2]

1 B.D. Price (ed.), *The Registers of Henry Scott Tuke (1858–1929)*, Falmouth: Royal Cornwall Polytechnic Society, 1983, no. R766.
2 Lucciani also sat for *Bathing Group* (1913), which Tuke presented to the Royal Academy as his Diploma Work and *Fawn*, exhibited in 1914. Information derived from Catherine Wallace sale notes for *Head of Nicola*, in Christie's 'Victorian & British Impressionist Art', 15 June 2011 (sale 7973, lot 43).

Cliffs and Breakers

1884
oil on wood
12.4 x 21.6 cm

Hunterian Museum
and Art Gallery,
University of Glasgow

The Bathing Posts, Brittany

1893
oil on wood
16.6 x 24.3 cm

Hunterian Museum
and Art Gallery,
University of Glasgow

James Abbott McNeill Whistler

1834–1903

Previously a remote and rarely visited location, St Ives had become easily accessible from London with the opening of the branch railway line from St Erth in 1877. It soon became a popular tourist destination, the first guide to the town being published in 1884.

Whistler stayed in St Ives from late December 1883 until early February 1884, accompanied by his followers Mortimer Menpes and Walter Sickert. He was preparing for an important exhibition of his work at Dowdeswell's Gallery in New Bond Street, which opened in May 1884 under the title 'Notes' – 'Harmonies' – 'Nocturnes'. In St Ives Whistler painted some 20 small oils and seven watercolours, at least nine of which were shown in the exhibition.[1] *Cliffs and Breakers* is probably the picture exhibited as *The Green Headland*. It shows the Carrick Du promontory at the west end of Porthmeor Beach at high tide.

The St Ives paintings returned Whistler to studying the sea, as he had first done in his Trouville paintings of 1865, working alongside Courbet. Initially Whistler had found St Ives dull, the countryside uninspiring and the sea limiting.[2] But he quickly changed his mind and in the letters he wrote that winter he indicated that the oils he was painting represented a new departure for him: 'I am doing things quite new down here of course – New eggs am I laying'.[3] The novelty he referred to was to work on a very small scale – oil sketches (pochades) on panel – to distil the essence of his response. Sickert said of them:

> Whistler expressed the essence of his talent in his little panels, *pochades*, it is true, in measurement, but masterpieces of classic painting in importance... The relation and keeping of the tones is marvellous in its severe restriction... He will give you in a space nine inches by four an angry sea, piled up, and running in, as no painter ever did before.[4]

The exhibition was deliberately limited to these very small works, exhibited in deep frames that required the viewer to scrutinise them from close range. The gallery walls were decorated in white and pale pink, the floor covered in white matting, all designed to set off the exhibits to maximum effect.

In the summer of 1893 Whistler spent six weeks in Brittany to paint seascapes. The resident St Ives artists had been nonplussed by Whistler's avoidance of the paraphernalia they considered essential: a big canvas, an easel, large brushes and a sketching umbrella.[5] In Brittany he was again among heavily-encumbered artists going out dutifully to sketch *en plein air*, but he complained that the hot weather, with its brassy sky and tin sea, was only suitable for tourists, not painters.[6] Nevertheless he produced seven oils including *The Bathing Posts, Brittany*. As in the St Ives works a decade earlier, the economy of means in this picture is striking, although here the animated sky, fast-moving yachts and play of light on the sea contribute to a less starkly reduced image.

1 A further dozen may have been produced in the town.
2 Letter to his sister-in-law Helen Whistler [January 1884], quoted in Anna Gruetzner Robins *A Fragile Modernism: Whistler and his Impressionist Followers*, New Haven and London: Yale University Press, 2007, p.13.
3 Letter to Ernest George Brown assistant manager at the Fine Art Society. Glasgow University Library, MS Whistler LB 9/17.
4 Walter Sickert 'The New Life of Whistler', *The Fortnightly Review*, 84, December 1908, pp. 1027–28.
5 Mortimer Menpes, *Whistler as I knew him*, London: A and C Black, 1904, pp.135–40.
6 Letters to David Croal Thomson and Joseph Pennell, 1/8 September 1893?. Library of Congress Manuscript Division, Pennell-Whistler Collection, PWC D/1/5; PWC 272/2/3.

List of works on display

Vanessa Bell (1879–1961)

Studland Beach
(verso: *Group of Male Nudes*
by Duncan Grant)
c.1912 | oil on canvas
Tate, London

Robert Polhill Bevan (1865–1925)

Green Devon
1919 | oil on canvas
Plymouth City Museum and Art Gallery

The Chestnut Tree
c.1916–19 | oil on canvas
The Ashmolean Museum, Oxford.
Presented by Robert Alexander Bevan,
the artist's son, 1957

Devonshire Valley, no. 1
c.1913 | oil on canvas
Royal Albert Memorial Museum
& Art Gallery

Culme valley, Devon
1913
black chalk with watercolour on paper
The Trustees of the British Museum.
Donated by Robert Alexander Bevan

An outhouse, Devon
black chalk with watercolour on paper
The Trustees of the British Museum.
Donated by Robert Alexander Bevan

A Breton valley
c.1894 | lithograph on paper
The Trustees of the British Museum

Poplars Brittany
c.1894 | lithograph on paper
The Trustees of the British Museum

Eugène Boudin (1824–98)

Deauville
1893 | oil on canvas
The Samuel Courtauld Trust,
The Courtauld Gallery, London.
On display at RAMM only

A Beach near Trouville
1895 | oil on canvas
The Trustees of the Barber Institute of
Fine Arts, University of Birmingham

Paul Cézanne (1839–1906)

View of a house through bare trees
drawing on paper
The Trustees of the British Museum.
Donated by Lord Clark of Saltwood

Les Grands Baigneurs
1896–98 | lithograph on paper
Pallant House Gallery

George Clausen (1852–1944)

Winter Work
1883–84 | oil on canvas
Tate, London

A Frosty March Morning
1904 | oil on canvas
Tate, London

An artist painting out of doors
1882 | oil on panel
Bristol's Museums, Galleries and Archives.
Presented by Hugh Clausen, the artist's son,
1949

Charles Conder (1868–1909)

Apple Blossom at Dennemont
1893 | oil on canvas
The Ashmolean Museum, Oxford.
Bequeathed by J.G. Legge through
The Art Fund, 1940

Wynford Dewhurst (1864–1941)

Summer Mist, Valley of La Creuse
c.1919 | oil on canvas
National Museum of Wales

John Duncan Fergusson (1874–1961)

Twilight, Royan
1910 | oil on board
Edinburgh, Scottish National Gallery
of Modern Art. Bequeathed by
Dr R.A. Lillie 1977

Stanhope Alexander Forbes (1857–1947)

The Convent
1882 | oil on canvas
Private lender

Study of a Fisherwoman
(study for *A Fish Sale on a Cornish Beach*)
1884 | oil on canvas
Penlee House Museum & Gallery

A Fish Sale on a Cornish Beach
1885 | oil on canvas
Plymouth City Museum and Art Gallery

Beach Scene – St Ives
1886 | oil on canvas
Bristol's Museums, Galleries and Archives

Paul Gauguin (1848–1903)

Joies de Bretagne
(*The pleasures of Brittany*)
1889 | lithograph on paper
The Trustees of the British Museum.
Bequeathed by Campbell Dodgson

Landscape at Pont-Aven
(ascribed to Paul Gauguin)
1888 | oil on canvas
The Trustees of the Barber Institute of
Fine Arts, University of Birmingham

Charles Ginner (1878–1952)

Clayhidon
1913 | oil on canvas
Royal Albert Memorial Museum
& Art Gallery

Spencer Frederick Gore (1878–1914)

Study for The Cinder Path
1912 | coloured chalks and graphite
The Trustees of the British Museum

The Beanfield, Letchworth
1912 | oil on canvas
Tate, London

The Cinder Path
1912 | oil on canvas
The Ashmolean Museum, Oxford.
Presented by Robert Alexander Bevan,
1957

Armand Guillaumin (1841–1927)

Les Pommiers à Damiette
1893 | oil on canvas
Aberdeen Art Gallery & Museums

Laura Knight (1877–1970)

The Beach
c.1908 | oil on canvas
Laing Art Gallery, Newcastle upon Tyne
(Tyne and Wear Archives and Museums).
On display at RAMM only

Henry Herbert La Thangue (1859–1929)

*The Boat Builder's Yard, Cancale,
Brittany*
1881 | oil on canvas
National Maritime Museum, London

Claude Monet (1840–1926)

The Museum at La Havre
1873 | oil on canvas
The National Gallery, London

The Church at Vétheuil
1880 | oil on canvas
Southampton City Art Gallery

Roderic O'Conor (1860–1940)

Yellow Landscape
1892 | oil on canvas
Tate, London

Samuel John Peploe (1871–1935)

Boats at Royan
1910 | oil on board
Edinburgh, Scottish National Gallery
of Modern Art. Bequeathed by
Dr R.A. Lillie 1977

Camille Pissarro (1830–1903)

*View of the Versailles Road,
Louveciennes*
1870 | oil on canvas
Southampton City Art Gallery

A Corner of the Meadow at Eragny
1902 | oil on canvas
Tate, London

Théorie de Baigneuses
1897
lithograph, on pale grey chine collé
The Trustees of the British Museum.
Donated by Charles Ricketts

Eragny: landscape with trees
1890 | watercolour on paper
The Trustees of the British Museum.
Donated by Charles Ricketts

Lucien Pissarro (1863–1944)

*Apple Blossom, Riversbridge Farm,
Blackpool*
1921 | oil on canvas
Royal Albert Memorial Museum
& Art Gallery

Pierre Auguste Renoir (1841–1919)

St Tropez
c.1893 | oil on canvas
Birmingham City Museum & Art Gallery

Moulin Huet Bay, Guernsey
c.1883 | oil on canvas
The National Gallery, London

Walter Richard Sickert (1860–1942)

Rushford Mill, Chagford
1916 | oil on canvas
Lent by the Syndics of the
Fitzwilliam Museum, Cambridge

Clodgy Point, Cornwall
1883–84 | oil on panel
Hunterian Museum & Art Gallery,
University of Glasgow

Alfred Sisley (1839–99)

La Petite Place – La Rue du Village
1874 | oil on canvas
Aberdeen Art Gallery & Museums

Bords de rivière / Les Oies
1897 | colour lithograph on paper
The Trustees of the British Museum.
Bequeathed by Campbell Dodgson

Philip Wilson Steer (1860–1942)

The Beach at Walberswick
c.1889 | oil on wood
Tate, London

Walberswick, Children Paddling
1891 | oil on canvas
Lent by the Syndics of the
Fitzwilliam Museum, Cambridge.

*Two girls on Walberswick Beach,
Suffolk*
c.1890 | oil on panel
Plymouth City Museum and Art Gallery

Henry Scott Tuke (1858–1929)

July Sun
1913 | oil on canvas
Royal Academy of Arts

James Abbott McNeill Whistler
(1834–1903)

Cliffs and Breakers
1884 | oil on wood
Hunterian Museum & Art Gallery,
University of Glasgow

The Bathing Posts, Brittany
1893 | oil on wood
Hunterian Museum & Art Gallery,
University of Glasgow

Acknowledgements

Notes on contributors

Dr Ysanne Holt is Reader in the History of Art at the University of Northumbria. She writes about early twentieth-century British art and about landscapes and cultures of ruralism. She is also editor of the Routledge journal *Visual Culture in Britain*.

Sam Smiles is Emeritus Professor of Art History at the University of Plymouth. He has published on British eighteenth and nineteenth-century art and its legacy and is a specialist on the works of J.M.W. Turner.

Thank you

The Royal Albert Memorial Museum & Art Gallery gratefully acknowledges the support and assistance of the following individuals:

David Anderson, the late Maureen Attrill, Alex Beard, Stephen Bemrose, Alison Bevan, Heather Birchall, Julie Blanks, Carol Brand, Stuart Brown, Christopher Brown, Chezzy Brownen, Aisha Burtenshaw, Julia Carver, Aarti Chanrai, Christina Chilcott, Catherine Clement, Griffin Co, Caroline Collier, Alison Cooper, Mary Costello, Clive Coward, Alison Cox, Tim Craven, R. John Croft, Rhiannon Davies, Patrick Elliott, Verity Elson, Richard Etienne, Lisa Evans, Sara Everett, Kevin Fewster, Julie Finch, Lucy Findley, Jane Fisher, Grant Ford, Geraldine Glynn, Harriett Graham, Anthony Griffiths, Claire Hallinan, Jane Hamilton, Tom Heaven, Katie Herbert, Rachel Hewitt, Sarah Hodge, Victoria Hogarth, Ysanne Holt, Emily Hope Thomson, Clara Hudson, Nancy Ireson, David Jaffé, Jenny Kinnear, Philippa Kirkham, John Leighton, Neil MacGregor, Marie-Therese Mayne, Sally McIntosh, Rita McLean, Julie Milne, Susan Morris, Jon Moulton, Pauline Moulton, Nicola Moyle, Edwina Mulvany, Anna Murray, Robert Owen, Ian Parfitt, Steven Parissien, Varshali Patel, Nicholas Penny, Timothy Potts, Stephanie Pratt, Christine Rew, Sarah Richardson, Katherine Richmond, Mary Rose Rivett-Carnac, Pamela Robertson, John Sansom, David Scrase, Ambrose Scott-Moncrieff, Nicholas Serota, Francesca Sidhu, Nicole Simões da Silva, Janice Slater, Clare Smith, Jane K Smith, Thyrza Smith, Chanté St Clair Inglis, Ann Stead, MaryAnne Stevens, Sheena Stoddard, Ann Sumner, Martin Thomas, Barbara Underwood, Ernst Vegelin, Caroline Villier-Stuart, Iain Watson, Val Webb.

This exhibition could not have been achieved without the agreement of significant public and private collections to lend their works and we would like to thank them all for their understanding and assistance.

A special thank-you to Sam Smiles and Penny Sexton whose contribution to the exhibition was fundamental and whose expertise has informed every aspect of the exhibition's realisation.

The Royal Albert Memorial Museum & Art Gallery would like to thank the Museum staff for all their hard work in bringing this exhibition to fruition.

Picture credits

Aberdeen Art Gallery
- Armand Guillaumin (1841–1927) *Les Pommiers à Damiette*
  © Aberdeen Art Gallery & Museums Collections
- Alfred Sisley (1839–1899) *La Petite Place*
  © Aberdeen Art Gallery & Museums Collections

Art Gallery and Museum Kelvingrove, Glasgow
- Jules Bastien-Lepage (1848-84) *Pauvre Fauvette*
  © Culture and Sport, Glasgow (Museums)

Ashmolean Museum, Oxford
- Robert Polhill Bevan (1865–1925) *The Chestnut Tree*
  © Ashmolean Museum, University of Oxford
- Charles Conder (1868–1909) *Apple Blossom at Dennemont*
  © Ashmolean Museum, University of Oxford
- Spencer Frederick Gore (1878–1914) *The Cinder Path*
  © Ashmolean Museum, University of Oxford

Barber Institute of Fine Arts, Birmingham
- Eugène Boudin (1824–1898) *A Beach near Trouville*
  © The Barber Institute of Fine Arts, The University of Birmingham
- Ascribed to Paul Gauguin (1848–1903) *Landscape at Pont-Aven*
  © The Barber Institute of Fine Arts, The University of Birmingham

Birmingham Museum and Art Gallery, Birmingham
- Pierre Auguste Renoir (1841–1919) *St Tropez*
  © Birmingham Museums & Art Gallery

Bristol Museum and Art Gallery, Bristol
- George Clausen (1852-1944) *An artist painting out of doors*
  © Estate of George Clausen. In the collection of Bristol City Museum and Art Gallery
- Stanhope Alexander Forbes (1857–1947) *Beach Scene – St Ives*
  © Bristol City Museum and Art Gallery, UK/ The Bridgeman Art Library

British Museum
- Robert Polhill Bevan (1865–1925) *A Breton valley*
  © The Trustees of the British Museum
- Spencer Frederick Gore (1878–1914) *Study for The Cinder Path*
  © The Trustees of the British Museum
- Jean-François Millet (1814-75) *Summer, The Gleaners*
  © The Trustees of the British Museum

Courtauld Institute of Art, London
- Eugène Boudin (1824–1898) *Deauville*
  © The Samuel Courtauld Trust, The Courtauld Gallery, London

Fitzwilliam Museum, Cambridge
- Walter Richard Sickert (1860–1942) *Rushford Mill, Chagford*
  © The Estate of Walter Richard Sickert 2011. All Rights Reserved, DACS. In the collection of the Fitzwilliam Museum, Cambridge
- Philip Wilson Steer (1860–1942) *Walberswick, Children Paddling*
  © Artist's Estate. In the collection of the Fitzwilliam Museum, Cambridge

Hunterian Museum, Glasgow
- Walter Richard Sickert (1860–1942) *Clodgy Point, Cornwall*
  © The Estate of Walter Richard Sickert 2011. All Rights Reserved, DACS. In the collection of the Hunterian Museum & Art Gallery, University of Glasgow
- James Abbott McNeill Whistler (1834–1903) *Cliffs and Breakers*
  © Hunterian Museum & Art Gallery, University of Glasgow
- James Abbott McNeill Whistler (1834–1903) *The Bathing Posts, Brittany*
  © Hunterian Museum & Art Gallery, University of Glasgow

Laing Art Gallery, Newcastle upon Tyne
- Laura Knight (1877–1970) *The Beach*
  © Reproduced with permission of The Estate of Dame Laura Knight DBE RA 2010. All Rights Reserved. In the collection of the Laing Art Gallery, Tyne and Wear Archives & Museums

National Gallery of Modern Art, Edinburgh
- John Duncan Fergusson (1874–1961) *Twilight, Royan*
  © The Fergusson Gallery, Perth & Kinross Council. In the collection of the Scottish National Gallery of Modern Art
- Samuel John Peploe (1871–1935) *Boats at Royan*
  © Scottish National Gallery of Modern Art

National Gallery, London
- Claude Monet (1840–1926) *The Museum at La Havre*
  © The National Gallery, London
- Pierre Auguste Renoir (1841–1919) *Moulin Huet Bay, Guernsey*
  © The National Gallery, London
- Vincent van Gogh (1853–90) *A Wheatfield with Cypresses*
  © The National Gallery, London

National Maritime Museum, London
- Henry Herbert La Thangue (1859–1929) *The Boat Builder's Yard, Cancale, Brittany* © National Maritime Museum, Greenwich, London

National Museum of Wales, Cardiff
- Wynford Dewhurst (1864–1941) *Summer Mist, Valley of La Creuse*
  © National Museum of Wales
- Alfred Sisley (1839–99) *The Cliff at Penarth, Evening, Low Tide*
  © National Museum of Wales

Penlee House Gallery and Museum, Penzance
- Stanhope Alexander Forbes (1857–1947) *Study of a Fisherwoman (study for Fish Sale on a Cornish Beach)*
  © Penlee House Gallery and Museum, Penzance, UK/ The Bridgeman Art Library

Plymouth City Museum and Art Gallery, Plymouth
- Robert Polhill Bevan (1865–1925) *Green Devon*
  © Plymouth City Museum & Art Gallery
- Stanhope Alexander Forbes (1857–1947) *A Fish Sale on a Cornish Beach*. Photo © Plymouth City Museum and Art Gallery, Plymouth, UK/The Bridgeman Art Library

- Philip Wilson Steer (1860–1942)
  Two girls on Walberswick Beach, Suffolk
  © Artist's Estate. Photo © Plymouth City Museum & Art Gallery

Private lender
- Stanhope Alexander Forbes (1857–1947) *The Convent*
  © private collection UK/The Bridgeman Art Library.
  Image courtesy of Sotheby's Picture Library

Royal Academy of Arts, London
- Henry Scott Tuke RA (1858–1929) *July Sun*
  © Royal Academy of Arts, London

Royal Albert Memorial Museum & Art Gallery
- Robert Polhill Bevan (1865–1925) *Devonshire Valley, no. 1*
  © Royal Albert Memorial Museum & Art Gallery, Exeter
- Charles Ginner (1878–1952) *Clayhidon*
  © Royal Albert Memorial Museum & Art Gallery, Exeter
- Lucien Pissarro (1863–1944)
  Apple Blossom, Riversbridge Farm, Blackpool
  © The Estate of Lucien Pissarro. In the collection of the
  Royal Albert Memorial Museum & Art Gallery, Exeter.

Scottish National Gallery, Edinburgh
- Paul Gauguin (1848–1903) *The Vision after the Sermon*
  © National Gallery of Scotland

Southampton City Art Gallery, Southampton
- Claude Monet (1840–1926) *The Church at Vetheuil*
  © Southampton City Art Gallery, Hampshire, UK/
  The Bridgeman Art Library
- Camille Pissarro (1830–1903) *Louveciennes*
  © Southampton City Art Gallery, Hampshire, UK/
  The Bridgeman Art Library

Tate, London
- Vanessa Bell (1879–1961) *Studland Beach*
  © Estate of Vanessa Bell, courtesy Henrietta Garnett.
  In the collection of the Tate
- George Clausen (1852–1944) *Winter Work*
  © Estate of George Clausen. In the collection of the Tate
- George Clausen (1852–1944) *A Frosty March Morning*
  © Tate, London, 2011
- Spencer Frederick Gore (1878–1914) *The Beanfield, Letchworth*
  © Tate, London, 2011
- Roderic O'Conor (1860–1940) *Yellow Landscape*
  © Tate, London, 2011
- Camille Pissarro (1830–1903) *A Corner of the Meadow at Eragny*
  © Tate, London, 2011
- Philip Wilson Steer (1860–1942) *Richmond Castle*
  © Tate, London, 2011
- Philip Wilson Steer (1860–1942) *The Beach at Walberswick*
  © Tate, London, 2011
- JMW Turner (1775–1851) *Norham Castle, Sunrise*
  © Tate, London, 2011

The Wallace Collection, London
- Jules Dupré (1811–89) *Crossing the Bridge*
  © By kind permission of the Trustees of the Wallace Collection,
  London